LOST
......
WORDS
......
OF LOVE

BY SUSAN KELZ SPERLING

LOST WOR

Clarkson Potter/Publishers
New York

D S O F 𝓛 O V E

ILLUSTRATED BY R. O. BLECHMAN

Copyright © 1993 by Susan Kelz Sperling. Illustrations copyright © 1993 by R. O. Blechman. All rights reserved. No part of this book may be reproduced or transmitted in any form or by any means, electronic or mechanical, including photo-copying, recording, or by any information storage and retrieval system, without permission in writing from the publisher. Published by Clarkson N. Potter, Inc., 201 East 50th Street, New York, New York 10022. Member of the Crown Publishing Group. Random House, Inc. New York, Toronto, London, Sydney, Auckland. CLARKSON N. POTTER, POTTER, and colophon are trademarks of Clarkson N. Potter, Inc. Manufactured in the United States of America. Design by Louise Fili. Library of Congress Cataloging-in-Publication Data. Sperling, Susan Kelz. Lost words of love/by Susan Kelz Sperling.—1st ed. Includes bibliographical references. 1. English language —Obsolete words. 2. Love — Terminology. 3. Love – Humor. I. Title. PE1667.S58 1993 422'.0207– dc20 92-3949 CIP ISBN 0-517-58793-9 First Edition 10 9 8 7 6 5 4 3 2 1

FOR JEANNETTE,

WITH LOVE AND THANKS FOR HER CARING,

HER SENSE OF HUMOR,

AND HER LOVE OF LANGUAGE,

PEOPLE, AND LIFE.

*H*ow does a word become lost?

Far from being static, language is a living organism that changes to fit the times, historically and culturally, with old words constantly declining in popularity and newer ones entering the lexicon. From the beginnings of English around the year 450, significant long-term occurrences, including invasions of foreigners into Britain, shifts of population, and advances in trade and communications, had a profound effect upon the language. During this evolution into the mix we call modern English, untold numbers of words passed completely out of use. By examining not only specific words used by ordinary people who lived in Britain between the tenth and nine-teenth centuries but also words spoken by common folk in America during the nineteenth and early twentieth centuries, we moderns can both uncover a past that was very alive and discover timeless themes still operative today that connect us to our larger cultural framework.

All of the words cited in *Lost Words of Love* are designated "rare," "obsolete," or "dialect" in the various sources listed in the bibliography. Some may still be in use in remote regions of Britain and rural America, depending on the insularity of those communities. While the focus here is on various aspects of love, the book perforce brings in words relating to life in general to fit the context. Because the number of sources on the subject of lost words is itself limited, and since nuance is an imprecise science to begin with, the author has exercised some latitude in interpretation when weaving these dated terms into modern speech, especially with words that have multiple, seemingly unrelated meanings that add confusion to their intrin-sic charms.

As for their charms, they are indeed many. For it's the charm of their surface sounds coupled with their hidden layers of meaning that makes lost words come alive. Certain obsolete words beg to be spoken aloud once again simply because of the attention-getting juxtaposition of their letters, so that the definitions become secondary to their eye-catching appeal. All the more fascinating it is for us moderns to realize that unusual-looking and strange-sounding words like *snool, wowf, melsh-dick, picking-hole, bedgang, slurg, dumb-wife,* and *zowerswopped* really were used in the past by people similar to ourselves.

In addition to their surface value, many words that were replaced by others more suited to their times appear as fresh and fitting as contemporary equivalents. Picture the *snout-fair,* or handsome, fellow, strutting about town in the 1600s, wearing both an air of confidence from his good fortune in being born to a life of leisure and a pair of fine shoes unsullied by rough labor, and see how his very demeanor could have led envious, suspicious, working-class folk to assign him the less-than-flattering epithet *smooth-booted,* maligning him as a phony opportunist. Help yourself to the evocative word *smick,* "to kiss," which could slip into a love song just as easily today as it did in the "Bagford Ballad" of the late 1600s: "You smack, you smick, you wash, you lick, you smirk, you swear, you grin." Similarly jaunty is the seventeenth-century verse in which fleshy, worldly clergy were described thus: "Abbots were fat and friars *frim.*" And see how perfectly adaptable to today is *unpregnant,* which Shakespeare expanded upon from its literal meaning of "unreceptive" to become "inept at business" and "unimaginative." Note also how appropriate even now are lost terms from a lover's fifteenth-century lament addressing his own pining and crying: "I *snirp,* I *snobb,* I *sneip* on snout." If only he could have *unpuckered*—or relaxed.

More charms inherent to lost words become apparent the more that one delves into those pertaining to customs not only indicative of their own time but also universal in nature. The tenth-century custom known as *bridelope* was the literal forerunner of elopement, during which the groom took off with his bride on a "bridal run," galloping (*hlaup* in Old Teutonic) from the place of the ceremony to the couple's new home. The custom persisted until the late 1800s in the north of England and Scotland in the form of a race in which all of the men in the wedding party raced on horseback or by foot from the marriage scene to the house. Undoubtedly, the bride and groom pledged their vows under a *care-cloth,* a square canopy named for the French *carré,* or square, held over their heads by four attendants while the couple symbolically prayed for the same protection and religious blessing of their union still invoked from higher powers today. Who knows if perhaps the groom might have eventually become the victim of his wife's nightly *curtain-sermon,* a harangue of criticism saved for bedtime? Would he have escaped to the place known as *stewed prunes* (the brothel), where these fruits were displayed on windowsills like business signs? For it was in these establishments that the proprietress, often called a stewed prune herself, kept prunes on hand as preventives and cures for diseases contracted on the premises. And might the wife have then sought the advice of the silent *dumb-wife,* the fortune-teller, on whom seventeenth-century villagers conferred prescient powers to fit their concept of the larger cosmic harmony that they could validate in even so hapless a soul? Timely and timeless, the stories hidden within layers of lost words are reason enough to bring them back to life.

There is even a kind of twisted charm to those lost words about which only a small shred of information has come to light. And it's that tiny morsel that makes one long for more. *Vaticide* is one such word. Not much more is in print other than that it meant "the murder of prophets or poets." And how that tidbit tantalizes! Another teaser, *tharm,* is defined in Johnson's *Dictionary* as "intestines 'twisted for several uses.'" Like what? How? Imagine! We can go so far and then go no further. More often than not, the stories hidden within words that have passed out of use must remain buried with them.

Digging into lost words allows us moderns to become smug when considering how far we might have come since the old days when common folk were supposedly preoccupied more with the mundane and predictable than with the loftier aspects of life. True, many of those early words depict a world centered on such immediate concerns as food, farming, and health. At the same time, a good number also reveal people's wrestling with the more impenetrable mysteries of religion, cycles in nature, and the ever-present attraction of one sex to the other. While our day-to-day habits may have changed, and so too the words that identified them, we find in lost words a reflection of ourselves—especially in the lost words of love.

Poems
······
and
······
Rounds

A Variation on Elizabeth Barrett Browning

. . . .

How do I love thee? Let me count thy FEAKS.   CURLS

I love thee to the FOUNCE and breadth and height   BOTTOM

My soul can GREEP, when GRUBBLING out of sight   GROPE FOR/ FEELING IN THE DARK

For the ends of being and ideal FRITH.   PEACE

I love thee to the level of GROPSING's   TWILIGHT

Most STILLWORTH need, by sun and GRAKING light.   PEACEFUL/ EARLY DAWN

I love thee freely, as men YERR for right;   SCREAM, HOWL

I love thee purely, as they FLURN at praise.   SNEER

I love thee with the FLESHMENT put to use   EXCITEMENT

In my old FREAMS and with my childhood's FRASKS.   RAGES/TRICKS

I love thee with a SEELIHEAD I seemed to lose   HAPPINESS

With my lost VAMPERS—I love thee with the breath,   SOCKS

FARLIES, FLODDER of my life! And if God choose'll,   WONDERS/ BLUBBERING, WEEPING

I shall but after lunch thee better SNOOZLE.   SNUGGLE

. . . .

THE LOVER, *STOGGED** IN *VOLO-NOLA***

. . . .

*M*y love is MEVERLY,   SHY, BASHFUL

I can't be bold;

I long to warm her NUDDLE   NAPE OF
                                                         THE NECK

When it's cold.

Her FOADING CRISPLES tempt me,   BEGUILING/
                                                         TENDRILS

Each GOORDY limb;   PLUMP, ROUND

Her AMORETS invite me—   LOVING
                                                         GLANCES

Come, be FRIM.   FORWARD

Yet when one SAY-WELL beckons,   COMPLIMENT

"Come and QUATCH,"   REVEAL
                                                         A SECRET

Unspoken UTTERWARTS   FURTHER
                                                         WARNINGS

Bid "HINK! Just watch!"   A CRY MEANING
                                                         "HALT!"

    *STUCK

**VACILLATION

13

At DEAD-LIFT and POTVALIANT,

A POINT OF DES-
PERATION/MADE
COURAGEOUS BY
DRINKING/PINE,
WITHER

Still I SNIRP;

Shall I COURT HOLY WATER?

FLATTER

Chance a WURP?

GLANCE

I yearn to FLUNGE and FRAMPLE

FLY AND
PLUNGE/
GOBBLE UP
DELICACIES

Her PULPATOONS;

But—I'm stogged in volo-nola,

Till she swoons.

. . . .

$\mathcal{W}$hat is STILLWORTH?

STILLWORTH means peaceful. Frequently a new parent's STILLWORTH nap ends with his newborn's YUX.

What is a YUX?

A YUX is a hiccup. A YUX works its way up from deep in the HEART-SPOON.

What is the HEART-SPOON?

The HEART-SPOON of one's body is the pit of the stomach. The HEART-SPOON of a tree trunk is located near its TWISSLE.

What is a TWISSLE?

A TWISSLE is the place where branches of a tree separate. A TWISSLE struck by lightning might eventually become DRICKSIE.

What is DRICKSIE?

DRICKSIE means rotted, as happens with timber. It's from DRICKSIE hiding places in the woods that MELSH-DICKS emerge at night.

What are MELSH-DICKS?

MELSH-DICKS are forest goblins. MELSH-DICKS stay under cover until TWATTER-LIGHT.

What is TWATTER-LIGHT?

TWATTER-LIGHT is twilight. It's especially romantic to hold hands with someone you love at TWATTER-LIGHT and watch a STILLWORTH sunset together.

THE LOVER, FINALLY UNSTOGGED

. . . .

*A*s close as CLOVES AND ORANGES,

Like KISSINGCRUSTS that touch,

Like FERNTICLES—a GREEP of them,

That's what I want so much.

SPICED FRUIT
ADDED TO
BREWING LIQUOR/
SIDES OF BAKED
GOODS STUCK TO-
GETHER IN OVEN
FRECKLES/BUNCH

ENTERBATHING in a FOODER,

Just the two of us;

SWINGLING in our RAVARY,

In FOGUE, TENTIGINOUS.

INTERMINGLED/
BIG WINE TUB

REELING, DIZZY/
FIT OF PASSION

ARDOR/FILLED
WITH LUST

What's this? You ope your MODESTY-PIECE!

Your GEASON GREADE undo!

You urge me, "Quick! Don't TARTLE!

Untie your SLOPS and STOO!"

BAND OF LACE ON
A SHIRT

WONDROUS/
BOSOM

HESITATE

BREECHES/
EXCLAMATION
MEANING "GO
FOR IT!"

I'm WOWF, MISLEEFUL, O VAFROUS one,

That we're so much alike;

Let's HALCH FOOT-HOT, and PRANGLE,

In LOVESHIP fast and FRIKE!

PARTIALLY DE-
RANGED/INCRED-
ULOUS/SLY

EMBRACE/HAST-
ILY/SQUEEZE
TIGHTLY
LOVEMAKING/
LUSTY

. . . .

WITH APOLOGIES TO THE BARD

. . . .

Shall I compare thee to a MISTRESS-PIECE? — FEMININE MASTERPIECE

Thou art more CLARTY and more ZOWERSWOPPED; — SLOVENLY/ILL-NATURED

UNSNOD PIMGENETS mark thy CHICHEVACHE; — ROUGH/RED PIMPLES/PINCHED FACE

KINGSEVIL's lease hath left its AFTERCLAPS. — ILLNESS/CONSEQUENCES

Sometime the GOUND and GLEET of GRANDGORE shine; — SECRETION/DISCHARGE/INFECTIOUS DISEASE

And oft thy BLETCHED complexion is BESPAWLED; — SPOTTY/SMEARED

And all those fair to FLABERKIN FORDWINE, — PUFFINESS/DECLINE

By WANWEIRD and my WALMING at thy VULT. — MISFORTUNE/NAUSEA/FACE

But *her* eternal summer shall not WROX, — BEGIN TO DECAY

Nor lose possession of her MUSKIN fair; — PRETTY FACE

Nor shall death brag to RAFF her in REGORT, — SWEEP UP/A GULF OR DEEP PLACE IN THE SEA

When in eternal lines to time she'll SKEER. — MOVE

So long as men can FLOIT and eyes can see, — WHISTLE

So long lives this, so "so long," dear, to thee.

18

. . . .

*W*hat is a CURTAIN-SERMON?
A CURTAIN-SERMON is a lecture that a wife delivers at bedtime to her mate. A CURTAIN-SERMON might involve SNOOLING for hours on end.

What is SNOOLING?
To SNOOL means to berate a person constantly until his spirit is broken. SNOOLING one's partner while cleaning house together doesn't help get a WHITCH packed.

What is a WHITCH?
A WHITCH is a big storage chest, like a coffin. A WHITCH is larger than a DRYFAT.

What is a DRYFAT?
A DRYFAT is a container for things that must not get wet. The outside of a DRYFAT is usually UNSNOD.

What is UNSNOD?
UNSNOD means rough to the touch. An UNSNOD YARNWINDLE would be hard to maneuver.

What is a YARNWINDLE?
A YARNWINDLE is a wooden, cross-shaped device used for winding yarn into a ball. It's very satisfying to let a special friend PRAG your YARNWINDLE.

What is PRAG?
To PRAG means to cram or to stuff. A resourceful husband might secretly PRAG his ears with cotton to drown out a CURTAIN-SERMON.

TIT FOR TAT

. . . .

A GANDERMOONER wooed a wench,   WOMAN-CHASER
                 WHOSE WIFE JUST
                 HAD A BABY
Lured her with a leering BLENCH;   SIDE-GLANCE

She responded to his ruse,

Bequeathed him a WINCHESTER GOOSE;   SEXUAL DISEASE

His wife learned quickly of his FRAMP,   REVELING

So well did MISLOOK leave its stamp.   SINFUL LOOKING

And now in BEDGANG WORBLES he,   CONFINEMENT TO
                 BED/WRITHES,
                 WRIGGLES
YERRING in his misery,   HOWLING

"No more a FRANION! I'll be pure!   RECKLESS
                 FELLOW
Take all my YELLOW-BOYS for a cure!"   GOLD COINS

. . . .

. . . .

*W*hat is a SLOCKSTER?

A SLOCKSTER is someone who steals another person's servants. A SLOCKSTER might try to sneak a servant in through his PICKING-HOLE.

What is a PICKING-HOLE?

A PICKING-HOLE is an opening in a barn to drop sheaves of corn through. Hovering over his PICKING-HOLE is impossible for a farmer in BEDGANG.

What is BEDGANG?

BEDGANG means being confined to bed with illness. Many people in BEDGANG seek relief through the services of a HOWDY-WIFE.

What is a HOWDY-WIFE?

A HOWDY-WIFE is a midwife. Visits by a HOWDY-WIFE often result from a RAVARY.

What is a RAVARY?

A RAVARY is a passionate encounter. Careful planning is needed to schedule a RAVARY during a NOONSCAPE.

What is a NOONSCAPE?

A NOONSCAPE is a break for lunch. Trying to relax during a short NOONSCAPE can be frustrating if others NURT in.

What is NURT?

To NURT means to push or butt, the way some animals do with their horns. A farmer who's been wronged will feel a lot better after letting his bull out of its pen to NURT a SLOCKSTER.

A Personals Ad by "Mr. Macho" à la Joyce Kilmer

. . . .

I think that I shall never see

A FRANION more SNOUT-FAIR than me,
> GALLANT FEL-
> LOW/HANDSOME

With ELF-LOCKS on my hairy chest,
> CURLS

To PRANGLE 'gainst a THUFTEN's breast.
> PRESS/MAIDEN

Are you a TIRE-WOMAN who can TOOZE
> HATMAKER/
> TEASE WOOL AND
> WEAVE

A HALF-CAP? Likes to BRINCH with booze?
> HEADBAND/
> DRINK TOASTS

Knows DILLIGROUT from ANGLE-TWATCH?
> THICK SOUP/
> DRINK MADE
> WITH GROUND-UP

Likes FUCUS and CHOPPINS that match?
> EARTHWORMS/
> ROUGE/HIGH-
> HEELED SHOES

A PALINGMAN, my KIBBO-KIFT
> DEALER IN EELS/
> PROOF OF
> STRENGTH

Is CRIZZLES from my LIGHT-BED shift;
> ROUGH, SUN-
> BURNED SKIN/
> SAILING DAYS

Blind dates are made by fools like me,

But who scores if he's MEVERLY?
> BASHFUL

. . . .

The Bridegroom's Lament at the Church, or A New Twist on the Refrain to Rudyard Kipling's "Gentlemen-Rankers," Also Known as "The Whiffenpoof Song"

. . . .

A half-marrow quatched, I've lost my bride,　　HUSBAND/
BETRAYED

Boo! Hoo! Hoo!

My paranymph lured her; they shabbed out the　　BEST MAN/
side,　　SNEAKED

Boo! Hoo! Hoo!

bridelope, pew-fellows, fooders at church,　　WEDDING CERE-
MONY/FRIENDS/
WINE CASKS

Canceled! Stood up! Left in the lurch!

God have mercy on us, the whole flurch!　　MULTITUDE

Boo! Hoo! Hoo!

No friking in tuxes, fried shirts, and gloves,　　LIVELY DANCING/
STIFF-FRONTED
SHIRTS

Boo! Hoo! Hoo!

No brinching from cups parcel-gilt with doves,　　MAKING TOASTS/
PARTLY GILDED

Boo! Hoo! Hoo!

Under the CARE-CLOTH ne'er to be kissed,

PULPATOONS, UNDERMEAL all dismissed,

God have mercy, the GLEEKMEN are pissed!

Boo! Hoo! Hoo!

. . . .

CANOPY HELD
OVER COUPLE

DELICACIES/
LUNCHEON

PROFESSIONAL
MUSICIANS

. . . .

What is a DUMB-WIFE?
A DUMB-WIFE is a fortune-teller. A DUMB-WIFE would be the right one to ask if one's future mate will be UNPREGNANT.

What is UNPREGNANT?
UNPREGNANT means inept at business. Both UNPREGNANT people and corporate types MISENGLISH about the same.

What is MISENGLISH?
To MISENGLISH means to use words wrongly. To correct those who MISENGLISH, a teacher often has to issue an UTTER-WART.

What is an UTTER-WART?
An UTTER-WART is a final warning. Most children learn from experience that a disobeyed UTTER-WART means no PULPATOONS.

What are PULPATOONS?
PULPATOONS are delicacies. PULPATOONS are hard for dieters to FLURN.

What is FLURN?
To FLURN means to scorn. Couples in love have fewer lines on their faces because they FLURN less and UNPUCKER more.

What is UNPUCKER?
To UNPUCKER means to relax. Lovers seeking privacy sometimes UNPUCKER on WOOSE.

What is WOOSE?
WOOSE is marshy ground. To avoid catching cold on wet WOOSE, it's a good idea to get a weather report from a DUMB-WIFE.

The following is a close approximation of a passage from Ecclesiastes, rendered in lost words having similar meanings.

To every thing there is a season, and a time
    to every purpose under the COSMOTECTURE: WORLD'S THIN COVER

A time to TIDDER, and a time to WROX;   PRODUCE OFFSPRING/ DECAY

A time to NURRY, and a time to RAFF VIGIDITY;   NOURISH/ GATHER UP/NEW VEGETATION

A time to ACHARNE, and a time to UNPUCKER;   THIRST FOR BLOOD/RELAX

A time to SNOOL, and a time to SAY-WELL;   CONSTANTLY CHIDE/COMMEND

A time to FLODDER, and a time to FRAMP;   WEEP/REVEL

A time to SNIRP, and a time to FRIKE;   PINE AWAY/ DANCE

A time to FLURN, and a time to ENTERBATHE;   SNEER/ INTERMINGLE

A time to HALCH, and a time to ABLUDE from
    halching;   EMBRACE/ REFRAIN

A time to GREEP, and a time to DRY-DITCH;   GROPE/LABOR IN VAIN

A time to SNOOZLE, and a time to SCOURSE;   SETTLE IN/SWAP

A time to TIFLE, and a time to TOOZE;   STIR UP DISORDER/ WEAVE

A time to TARTLE, and a time to MORN-SPEAK;　　HESITATE/
　　　　　　　　　　　　　　　　　　　　　　　　DISCUSS

A time to engage in LOVESHIP, and a time to show　　MAKING LOVE/
　　MALE TALENT;　　　　　　　　　　　　　　　ILL WILL

A time for EXCARNIFICATION, and a time for FRITH.　　TEARING TO
　　　　　　　　　　　　　　　　　　　　　　　　PIECES/PEACE

. . . .

*W*hat is STIG?

STIG means shy and wary of being hurt. Trying to make conversation on a blind date can make a STIG person HINK.

What is HINK?

To HINK means to falter. It's natural to HINK if a romantic stroll in the moonlight is suddenly interrupted by thunder that booms like GLOX.

What is GLOX?

GLOX is the sound of liquid being shaken in a barrel. GLOX is welcome in a busy tavern where the servers are FRIM.

What is FRIM?

FRIM means vigorous and in good shape. Love has a way of making a person feel FRIM even if his every FEAK has fallen out.

What is a FEAK?

A FEAK is a curl. Finding a gray FEAK does not mean that one's entire body is about to WROX.

What is WROX?

To WROX means to begin to decay. Seeing his May romance WROX by September can make a lover WOWF.

What is WOWF?

WOWF means partly deranged. A WOWF animal on the loose might need a YACK to quiet him down.

What is a YACK?

A YACK is a hit on the head. The YACK that Sir Isaac Newton felt probably made him STIG of apple trees for the rest of his life.

ADVICE
......
TO THE
......
LOVELORN

Dear Millicent AIMCRIER, — ADVISER

    I have an ugly WAM on one cheek that DRETCHES — SCAR/UPSETS
me whenever I go to a party. And I don't like my
MURFLES, either. I've tried THEEKING them with all — FRECKLES/ COVERING
sorts of creams and lotions that haven't worked.
Can you please recommend something?

CARKED — ANXIOUS

Dear Carked,

    Have you tried FUCUS? It's actually a very old — ROUGE MADE FROM ROCK PLANTS
remedy that stays on the skin longer than ordinary
makeup, and you can PURFLE your fingernails with — DECORATE
it, as well. A good pharmacist should be able to mix
up some for you. You might also consider FARDRY, a — WHITE FACE PAINT
heavier covering, if you know in advance that you'll
be partying where the lights will be low.

Dear Millicent Aimcrier,

    My boyfriend's FLESH-SPADES are always CLARTY. — FINGERNAILS/ FILTHY
No matter how tactful I try to be, whenever I
mention this to him, he works himself into FARIES — AGITATED FITS
and won't listen to me. How do I get him to clean up
his act?

THRUNCHED, — ANNOYED
Joanne

Dear Joanne,

    Make the most of your next romantic time
together by giving your YOUNGHEDE a loving — BOYFRIEND
manicure. Carry a DENTISCALP with you in secret. — TOOTHPICK
While you are looking adoringly at his face and
EYEBITING him, gently take hold of one of his hands — BEWITCHING
and offer to perform some DEVILSHINE on him. — MAGIC

Keep up the eye contact as you reach for your concealed dentiscalp. Stroke each finger lovingly as you deftly wipe away the SPISS accumulation under each nail. He's sure not to mind receiving your message conveyed in such a tactile, pleasurable way.

Dear Millicent Aimcrier,

I'm really AT DEAD-LIFT about what to do. I'm married to the most GEASON woman in the world whom I wouldn't want to CLAPPERCLAW for a MISDEEDY she can't help. But last week at a Chinese restaurant our COPESMATES wound up again with WALMING because of the way she PRAGS piles of food into her mouth all at once, even using her LEECH-FINGER to cram in every tiny MANNERS-BIT. What's worse is that she keeps on talking while she's CHANKING so that CLARTS of food start dribbling out of the corners of her mouth and onto her chin. The poor woman next to her wound up getting BESPAWLED when she couldn't SKEER away and some GLEET landed right on her BULL-TOUR. So I tried to make a FRASK out of it. You know those paper umbrellas that sometimes come with a GOTCH of CLAMBERSCULL? I moved mine back and forth like a TALEVACE in front of the woman's VULT, but my wife, in her SEELIHEAD, didn't get the point. I wanted to THRID in the wall and die. What to do?

Caring but Confused

Marginal glosses:

- THICK
- DESPERATE
- WONDERFUL
- SCOLD
- WRONGDOING
- FRIENDS
- NAUSEA/PACKS IN
- ONE NEXT TO LITTLE FINGER/LAST PIECE LEFT ON PLATE/CHOMPING NOISILY/BIG CLUMPS/SPATTERED WITH SALIVA/MOVE QUICKLY/STICKY STUFF/FRIZZY HAIR PILED ON FOREHEAD/JOKE
- JUG
- STRONG ALE
- SHIELD/FACE
- INNOCENCE
- SLIDE THROUGH A NARROW PASSAGE

Dear C but C,

With the utmost reassurance that you mean no MALE TALENT, explain to your wife that others are being affected by her PARBREAKING. Ask her if she's having a problem with her WEEZLE. If that's not a factor, then delicately suggest experimenting with a few WALKING-SUPPERS—just the two of you. You might don a SUCKENY before she begins to eat. Guide her in slowing down her pace, starting with simple items like fruit. But watch what she does with the SCORK. Then proceed to more fancy dishes, like FLAMMICK. Remember, too, that your constant AMORETS will encourage her to break these unpleasant habits so that no WANWEIRD will occur at the next TUTTING.

> ILL WILL
> SPEWING SALIVA
> WINDPIPE
>
> MEALS AT WHICH DISHES GO AROUND TABLE FOR EACH PERSON TO CARVE/ SMOCK
> APPLE CORE
> DESSERT MADE OF BUTTER, EGGS, AND CHEESE/ LOVING GLANCES/ MISFORTUNE/ TEA PARTY FOR WOMEN

Dear Millicent Aimcrier,

I am MALLY of a man with a rough BUGLE-BEARD that gives me MERRY-GALLS whenever we're in a long embrace. How do I preserve my FAIRHEAD and my love life at the same time?

                    PITCHKETTLED in Pittsburgh

> FOND/SHAGGY BEARD/CHAFING SORES
> BEAUTY
>
> PUZZLED

Dear Pitchkettled,

This is one GARBOIL that, unfortunately, only you can resolve, for the right answer is whatever will work best for you. Since I gather that your friend doesn't intend to shave off his PAGGLING FEAKS, you are forced to face the TEENFUL truth: Can you speak to him openly about how his beard gives you MORMALS? Might the relationship perhaps deepen from your taking this important step to discuss your WONDSOME concerns together?

> STATE OF CONFUSION
>
> HANGING/CURLS
> TROUBLING
>
> INFLAMED SORES
>
> DIFFICULT

Dear Millicent CYMBAL-DOCTOR Aimcrier:

Just who do you think you are?

I'm "PITCHKETTLED," the one who wrote to you a while back about the MERRY-GALLS I was getting from my boyfriend's BUGLE-BEARD. But by the time your answer was printed, he'd already done a great job of FOADING me, convinced me to have a RUSH RING, and made me pregnant. Then your SMICKLY reply came out in the paper, saying I should openly tell him about my GARBOIL over the MORMALS his FEAKS were giving me because then "might the relationship perhaps deepen?" Are you FRASKING me? I'd really like to YACK you with a POPES-HEAD! Sure I went and told him what you wrote, and he got up and left me just before my GOOD-HOUR. So now I've got this YERRING baby that YOSKES all over my MARRY-MUFF, my HALF-MARROW's gone, and I have a VULT full of PIMGENETS and WATER-GALLS from FLODDERING all the time. You turned me into a CHICHEVACHE! I got so WOWF I even tried the FUCUS and FARDRY you suggested to another reader. They didn't work. My HOWDY-WIFE thought maybe FOREBROADS would cure BUBUKLES. But it didn't.

Then the FULYEAR had the nerve to come back two months after the baby was born, just to COURT HOLY WATER. He even suggested that my SAUCE-FLEME was what gave *his* son a bad case of RED-GOWN and that I couldn't even NURRY the kid because of my MISDIET. Then he took off again after he FREAMED an UTTER-WART that I'd better stop CHUNTERING and follow the advice of the doctor he was sending to VEY the baby. The doctor came and stuck some LOP-LOACHES on my son, gave

---

Marginal glosses:

- EMPTY-HEADED TEACHER
- PUZZLED
- SORES
- SHAGGY BEARD
- BEGUILING / "WEDDING" WITH NO OFFICIAL CEREMONY / SMART / DISTRESS / SORES
- CURLS
- TRICKING
- HIT / LONG-HANDLED BROOM
- LABOR / SCREAMING / HICCUPS / DRESS / HUSBAND / FACE / PIMPLES / RINGS AROUND EYES / CRYING / UGLY COW / DERANGED / ROUGE / WHITE FACE PAINT / MIDWIFE / MILK FROM COWS AFTER CALVING / PIMPLES
- ROGUE / TAKE ADVANTAGE / FACIAL SWELLING FROM SALT / SKIN ERUPTIONS / NOURISH / IMPROPER FEEDING
- GROWLED / FINAL WARNING / COMPLAINING
- EXAMINE
- LEECHES

33

me SMERLES to put on him, and told me to try
using EARTHAPPLE slices on myself.

  Now my BELLY-FRIEND has FORDWINED for good,
and I'm a WIDOW-BEWITCHED, while you're still at
your MURLIMEWS, "helping" your readers. JERNIE!
See what you got me into? So what other great
advice do you have? That I should UNPUCKER?

Pitchkettled, now QUATCHED

Margin glosses: OINTMENT / CUCUMBER / INSINCERE FLATTERER / VANISHED / WOMAN SEPARATED FROM MATE / FOOLISH ANTICS / AN OATH / RELAX / BETRAYED

Dear Pitchkettled, now Quatched,

  Millicent Aimcrier tries to help her public IN
PUDDING TIME with general answers to their
problems and does her best not to CLOINTER on very
complex situations and personalities. She hardly
derives MISDELIGHT or gloats over unpredictable and
painful circumstances her readers may encounter.
She wishes she could be a FATILOQUIST and predict
that a magical SPOORN would remove MALE
JOURNEYS forever. Life has dealt you heavy
FLABERKINS indeed from which you are SWINGLING.
The question now is how to get past this
SEEKSORROW state to discover the finer FARLIES of
life that you deserve. Millicent Aimcrier has great
faith in your strength of purpose. Perhaps a
QUESTMONGER can help direct your FOGUE and get
the NURVIL to pay. She dearly hopes that, like RAW-
HEAD, you too will rise to the top and feel quatched
no more.

Margin glosses: IN THE NICK OF TIME / TREAD HEAVILY / PLEASURE IN DOING SOMETHING WRONG / FORTUNE-TELLER / PHANTOM / BAD DAYS / BLOWS / REELING / MASOCHISTIC / WONDERS / PROSECUTOR / FURY / MISER / CREAM RISING TO SURFACE OF RAW OR UNHEATED MILK

PLAYLETS

......

THE CURTAIN-SERMON

. . . .

*C*haracters: The "unstogged" couple depicted earlier in the poem on pages 16 and 17, now married for 25 years

Place: Bed

Time: 2 A.M.

SHE: I thought I heard a FRAGOR.   LOUD NOISE

HE: Hmmmm . . . probably a MOLDWARP outside.   MOLE
Go back to sleep.

SHE: No, I really did. Like maybe from the
WORMSTALL.   OUTDOOR
                                                    SHELTER

HE: Mmmmmmm. Zzzzzz.

SHE: Well? You going to look?

HE: Huh? Wha? Nuh, wait till GRAKING. Shhhh.   EARLY DAWN

SHE: I can't sleep.

HE: What now? More noises?

SHE: Sort of. Well, more like STILLICIDE. Did you   WATER
                                                    DRIPPING
empty the WATERGANG?   TRENCH FOR
                                                    DRAINING
HE: Yuh, it's fine, hardly filled. Go back to sleep. OVERFLOW

SHE: I told you: I can't sleep. How can you sleep   SUPPER FOR
after eating so much at the REARING-FEAST?   WORKMEN AFTER
                                                     A ROOF-RAISING
I've still got the YUX. Must be something I   HICCUPS
ate. I thought the HOLLOW-WARE tasted
REEZED. Did you like my VOIDEE?   CHICKENS AND
                                                     RABBITS/
                                                     SCORCHED/
                                                     FANCY TIDBITS

HE: Ummm, sure, very FRIM, fine. Sshhh. — JUICY

SHE: Well, I gave the last SKILFERS to the dogs. . . . Are you going out there to see about that noise? — SMALL PIECES

HE: What?

SHE: I hear BRUSTLES. I'll get your SCATCHES. — CRACKLING NOISES/STILTS

HE: Go out? No! I'm tired! We've got two horses with PURSICKNESS that'll be KELKING again in a couple of hours, and I need some sleep! — LUNG AND GAS PROBLEMS/BELCHING

SHE: Well, you sure weren't thinking about sleep when that TUMBESTER came popping out of her POWDERING TUB! I saw you staring at her HEART-SPOON, all right! — FEMALE TUMBLER/BIG VAT FOR SALTING MEAT/NAVEL

HE: Oh, is that what all this is about? Okay, now I'm up. Wanna SANN? — ARGUE

SHE: All I asked was for you to go and see what's YERRING outside. I even offered to bring you your scatches so your feet wouldn't get QUEACHY in the BEAU-TRAPS. But oh, no, that's hardly worth getting out of bed for— certainly not as exciting as watching Miss HOTCH-HOTCH QUAGGLE around the SHINICLE in her skinny CHOPPINS! — MAKING LOUD NOISES / WET/LOOSE STONES IN FOOTPATHS / SHAKE-SHAKE/QUIVER LIKE JELLY/BONFIRE/HIGH-HEELED SHOES/VERBALLY BEATEN

HE: So now I'm getting BATTERFANGED about the entertainment at a party?

SHE: You even stuck your LEECH-FINGER up her BUMROLL! — ONE NEXT TO LITTLE FINGER/HIP PADDING UNDER SKIRT

HE: Just like all the other HALF-MARROWS!   HUSBANDS
Tucking in YELLOW-BOYS, that's all! You saw!   GOLD COINS
So what?

SHE: So go live with them and see how you and
that dear little MELSH-DICK of yours stand   FOREST GOBLIN
up!

HE: Very nice. FREAMING at me about   SCREAMING
MISDEEDIES and throwing my grandmother's   WRONGDOINGS
NIASSY bedtime stories at me at the same   ODDBALL
time. Real nice.

SHE: Poor MAMMOTHREPT! Can't go outside his   SPOILED BABY
own house to see if any HAMESUCKEN's going   ASSAULT ON
on. Big KIBBO-KIFT!   ONE'S HOUSE/
    PROOF OF
    STRENGTH/BIG
HE: Fine, Miss CLAPDISH! I'm going. JOLLOP!   MOUTH/SQUAWK-
You sure know how to LIB a guy, even if he's   ING CRY OF A
only having harmless fun like all the   TURKEY/
others. . . . Where are my VAMPERS?   CASTRATE

    SOCKS

SHE: Here. I have them. . . . I'm sorry. I shouldn't
SNOOL you like that. You're right. It was just   PICK ON
a party. I'll go outside with you. Maybe we
can take care of this WITH A WET FINGER.   EASILY
And then maybe when we come back upstairs,
we can SMICK and make up.   KISS

HE: Okay. Here, take my hand down the
GREEZE. . . .   FLIGHT OF
    STAIRS

SHE: Hello, Mr. MELSH-DICK, is it? I'm
MS. DEEDEE, and I'm so pleased to be signing
you up with our BEAU-TRAPS Dating Service.
You'll be so MISLEEFUL when you discover
how many MEAT-GIVING women will be
contacting you after all your data are
assembled—and you've paid all your
BUNGDOWNS, of course. Now, I'd like to
SKEER through this form that you filled out,
if that's all right with you.

FOREST GOBLIN

VAR. ON
MISDEEDY—A
WRONGDOING/
LOOSE
PAVEMENT/
INCREDULOUS/
HOSPITABLE

MONEY (COPPER
COINS)/RUN

NM: Oh, okay. Whatever you like.

DD: I see that your first name is NURVIL, Mr.
Melsh-dick. Is that what you wish to be
called? Or is there a nickname you prefer?
Like Nurr? Or NURRY? Or Nurv?

MISER OR
DWARFISH
PERSON

NOURISH

NM: Oh, I don't know about that. . . . Nobody's
ever called me anything but Nurvil all my
life. Does it matter?

DD: Well, that's really up to you. So maybe we
can get back to it. I see that you give your
occupation as, um, a PALINGMAN. Can you
describe that more fully so that our women
subscribers can respond to what it is you do?

DEALER OF
EELS

NM: I sell eels. They're really quite nice. They're
not GLEETY, and they're kind of a pretty
GOORDY shape, and they don't WORBLE too
much.

SLIMY

ROUND AND
PLUMP/
WRIGGLE

DD: What do you do with them?

NM: I RAFF them from their REGORT, and then I
sell them.

GATHER/DEEP
PLACE IN SEA

DD: Well, Mr. Melsh-dick—or may I call you
Nurvil?—some of our clients prefer to date
men in professions with more of a, shall we
say, SMOOTH-BOOTED image? Could you
perhaps find a way to make your job sound
more FRIM on this form? Or we can get back
to this later too. Now, about these hobbies
you listed—it's terrific to read here that you
like to cook! Women really go for a guy who
wants to make a big BOUFFAGE for them.
Could you write down some specific dishes
you like to prepare?

FLATTERING

JUICY

SATISFYING
MEAL

NM: Sure! I like to make melted cheese
sandwiches, though sometimes they come out
a little REEZED. And soup. I love soup.

SCORCHED

DD: Do you mean those fabulous soups with
everything in them? Real thick, like
DILLIGROUT?

HEARTY
VEGETABLE
STEW

NM: Well, not really, more like, uh, you know
those cans in the store with the red-and-
white labels? I like those. But the things I
make that I'm most proud of are my
SUMMER-CASTLES of Jell-O. You have to slide
all the different colors into place just IN
PUDDING TIME, or they won't stack right.

TOWERS

IN THE NICK
OF TIME

DD: Oh, I see. Um, Mr. Melsh-dick, one of the
questions on this form asks you to describe

the kind of woman you'd like to meet, but you left that blank. Don't you have some qualities in mind that you'd like to list?

NM: Uh, well, I'm kind of VOLO-NOLA on that. I'm not really sure. They're all okay. And I thought if I VEYED every little detail, then maybe the women would FLURN me, so I left it blank.

> "YES I DO, NO I DON'T"
>
> EXAMINED
>
> SCORN

DD: Then can you suggest something you might like to do together besides make soup? So we can match you up with COPESMATES, you see?

> COMPANIONS

NM: Oh, okay. Um, I don't get to do it very often, but I like to FRIKE. Is that all right?

> DANCE

DD: Great! Wow! Mr. Melsh-dick, I mean Nurv, I didn't expect you to say dancing! Like, what kinds are your favorites?

NM: Well, I do a pretty good LAVOLT. And the lambada.

> LIVELY, BOUNCING DANCE

DD: The lambada? Talk about first impressions! Tell me, Nurv, did you bring a recent photograph of yourself? Or do you want us to take one of you right here? That'll be 25 YELLOW BOYS extra, you realize.

> GOLD COINS

NM: Uh, no, I mean, well, uh, I guess I'm still TARTLING about that, I mean, uh, no, I didn't bring a picture with me. And I'm not too sure I want to take one here since I'm

> HESITATING

feeling some WALMING in my HEART-SPOON NAUSEA/PIT OF STOMACH
just now. Do I have to have a photo? Can I
still sign up without one?

DD: Well, if you prefer. Okay, Nurvil, if you could
please finalize this form and leave me your
bungdowns, then I'll PRAG all your STUFF
information into our computer. I bet it'll
come up with quite a list! There's lots of
FLESHMENT ahead for you! EXCITEMENT

NM: Oh, okay.

LOVE
......
LETTERS

Dear Betsy,

I cannot get your MUSKIN out of my mind. Your every little FERNTICLE FRIKES before my eyes. Remember our LAVOLT on the FAIRY-CIRCLE last GO-SUMMER? It wasn't just the PETER-SEE-ME that made me POTVALIANT. It was your delicious DORLOT and those PAWKY looks you gave me now and then. And remember when we slipped on the WOOSE and your BUMROLL got all QUEACHY? And then you let me lift you into the TWISSLE, where you caught your LEECH-FINGER on a GRIBBLE? I loved SMICKING it and hearing you say, "All better." I wanted to SKEER with you to the SUMMER-CASTLE right then and there, but I realized we'd have to NOGGLE a long way up there. When we RAFFED instead on that YELM I found, I was MISLEEFUL at having you all to myself. It was after that fellow came by and squeezed us into his TIMWHISKY and brought me back to my rooms and you back to your aunt's house that I knew you were the one I'd want to TIDDER with forever. Please say you might feel the same. Meantime, I'm sending you this SARPE as a token of my love. Will you SCOURSE something of yours with me? I'll be SNIRPING away until I have your answer!

Yours,
John

PRETTY FACE/
FRECKLE/
DANCES/LIVELY
DANCE/LAWN/
AUTUMN/
SPANISH WINE/
EXCITED/KNOT OF
HAIR ON
FOREHEAD/SLY/
MARSHY
GROUND/SKIRT
BUSTLE/WET/
TREE TRUNK
WHERE
BRANCHES
MEET/ONE NEXT
TO LITTLE
FINGER/TREE
SHOOT/KISSING/
RACE/TOWER/
WALK
AWKWARDLY/
HUDDLED/
STRAW/
INCREDULOUS/
ONE-HORSE
CARRIAGE

HAVE CHILDREN

GOLD NECKLACE

SWAP

PINING

Dear John,

I will never forget the night we two FRAMPED together last go-summer. Thank you for the beautiful sarpe, but I have to send it back to you. I hope you understand that I bear you no MALE TALENT in saying that LOVESHIP with you is not what I intended. Another FRANION has entered my life. In fact, it's the same one who picked us up in his TIMMY-WHISKY (that's what he calls it) that night.

After we dropped you off, we didn't go straight to my aunt's. He asked me if I wanted to get more comfortable and fluffed up his BANKERS. He invited me to warm up under his enormous FOOT-CLOTH. Then we finished off some HEEL-TAPS he found and got to talking. Turns out he's a CATER-CAP and now a DOUBLE READER who doesn't mind getting BLETCH on his hands, too. When we got to my aunt's, he offered me his arm as I KEVVELED down the GREEZE and gave me a soft SASHOON.

Since that night, Reggie and I have been riding around and FLOITING a lot of love songs in his carriage, so I really can't keep your sarpe any longer.

I think you should know, too, that it's because your SLOPS GUMBLED so much to begin with that I tripped on them and fell that night, and now my leg will take a long time to heal. By the way, if you want to look really SNARP, maybe you should get a great MIDDLEGOOD WRAP-RASCAL like Reg's. And you know those PAWKY looks you thought I was giving you? They really were IRPS I was making to hide the LIFEBLOOD I've had since childhood.

REVELED

ILL WILL

MAKING LOVE

GREAT FELLOW

SAME AS
TIMWHISKY

CUSHIONS

DECORATED
HORSE COVER/
REMAINS LEFT IN
LIQUOR BOTTLE/
UNIVERSITY
GRADUATE/
LAWYER IN SEC-
OND TERM OF
STUDY/BLACK
AXLE GREASE/
WALKED
CLUMSILY/STEPS/
LEATHER PAD TO
WEAR INSIDE
BOOT/WHISTLING

BREECHES/FIT
LOOSELY

SHARP

LINEN/LOOSE
OVERCOAT/
SLY/BODY CON-
TORTIONS

EYELID TIC

I hope this doesn't HOTCH you up too much. You really are a SWEEKING guy, and I mean that from the FOUNCE of my heart.

SHAKE
SWINGING
BOTTOM

Fondly,
Betsy

Dear Rapunzel,

Help!

It's barely GRAKING, I'm halfway up to your DREAM-HOLE in the SUMMER-CASTLE, and I caught my SURPEACH on a GRIBBLE! Can you let down your ELF-LOCKS FOOT-HOT?

EARLY DAWN
WINDOW SLIT TO ADMIT LIGHT/ TOWER/JEWELED ORNAMENT ON TURBAN/TREE SHOOT/CURLY HAIR/FAST/ SHAKY

TEALT but hanging on,
Your Prince

Dear Prince,

What do I do about my mother, the TAISCH? I'd love nothing more than to be the usual MEAT-GIVER I am and to THRID you through my dream-hole WITH A WET FINGER right now, but she just YERRED at me never to see you again—or else! GRUBBLE down to the TWISSLE around at the back, and as soon as it's safe, I'll FLOIT and FLUNGE you my FEAKS!

PHANTOM
HOSPITABLE PERSON/SLIDE THROUGH NAR- ROW PASSAGE/ EASILY/YELLED/ GROPE
TREE TRUNK WHERE BRANCHES MEET/ WHISTLE/FLING/ CURLS

STOGGED,
Rapunzel

STUCK

Dear Juliet,

Let's you and me SHAB OUT tonight and have some fun! I hear there's a great party we can INKLE in on down at the WORMSTALL. It's already almost EVEGLOM, so tell your THUFTEN that you're going to visit the Friar, and when you hear a FLURCH of nightingales—not larks, but nightingales for sure—meet me at that big DRYFAT near the BEAU-TRAPS, and we'll lark the whole night long.

SMICK, smick,
Romeo

P.S. Just thinking about your NUDDLE makes my FLESHMENT enormous. Can I rub it again tonight?

SNEAK AWAY / ATTEND WITHOUT INVITATION / OUTDOOR SHELTER / TWILIGHT / MAID BUNCH

BARREL / LOOSE PAVEMENT IN FOOTPATH KISS

NECK

EXCITEMENT

Dear Romeo,

I'm so HOTCHED! Today was the one day every year that my parents have a DUMB-WIFE come over, so we all watched her do her awesome ASS-RIDDLIN under the LOVET, just like always. But this time, suddenly an enormous PRESTER blew the ashes all over the place! And when they settled down into the SLUT-GRATE, the shape of my shoes appeared! I'm totally WOWF! O Romeo, can you help me NURT this awful BULL-BEGGAR out of my mind?

SHOOK UP

FORTUNE-TELLER / ASH-SIFTING TO PREDICT FATE / ROOF OPENING / BURNING WHIRLWIND / HEARTH / DERANGED / PUSH / OBJECT DESIGNED TO SCARE PERSON

Tonight!
Juliet

49

Dear Penelope,

This may sound MISLEEFUL, but a FATILOQUIST on one of these islands gave us an UTTER-WART today that a terrible THODE would rise, bringing us only WANWEIRD from now on. I sure hope not, since a few crew members are already so sick with WALMING that they're hanging over the side every few minutes. How are things at home? Are those TENTIGINOUS visitors proving WONDSOME? Remember, I intend to keep my promise never to be DOUBLE-TONGUED, although there are some mighty NIASSY FARLIES going on wherever we go.

Love,
Odysseus

UNBELIEVABLE/
FORTUNE-TELLER/
WARNING/
VIOLENT WIND

MISFORTUNE

NAUSEA

LECHEROUS/
TROUBLESOME

DECEITFUL

WILD/STRANGE
THINGS

Dear Odysseus,

You've written me only once during the five weeks you've been away, and you sure don't seem to be making any great effort to call me ship to shore, so don't expect me to SNIRP away here, just waiting to hear from you. Your royal GARBAGER has turned the palace into a FREAMING FLESH-SHAMBLES and gotten us ten FLITWITES already. Your SNOUT-FAIR attendants act more like EYE-WAITERS now that you're gone, SLURGING around and STROATING on PETER-SEE-ME and PULPATOONS. I'm even more ZOWERSWOPPED because I don't know for sure yet if I'm HEAVY-FOOTED. Don't worry, it couldn't be anyone but you. Look, I'd never turn you into a SUMMER'S BIRD, but I don't want to be HIPPOED either. I've had enough of the weaving and ripping-

PINE

KITCHEN
OFFICER/
ROARING/
BROTHEL/FINES
FOR BRAWLING/
HANDSOME/
SERVANTS WHO
WORK ONLY WHEN
WATCHED/LYING
SLUGGISHLY/
FILLING UP/
WINE/DELI-
CACIES/ILL-
NATURED/
PREGNANT/
CUCKOLD/
DECEIVED

out routine, so now that I've spent an hour alone with my WAZE, the WATER-CASTER's taking me out for a ride on a BROWNSWINE.

CUSHION BEHIND HEAD/URINE TESTER FOR ILLS/ PORPOISE

> Love,
> Penelope

Dear Dulcinea,

Good news! I found a cure for Rosinante's PURSICKNESS. All I did was mix a FRUNDEL of barley with AXUNGER and have the horse lie in a POWDERING-TUB of it for a week. It seemed to do the FRASK, though maybe just getting her off the WOOSE helped, too. I've been removing a lot of people's MALE MORTES these days. The villagers really trust me as their PISS-PROPHET! So many of them who once stared FORTHFARE in the VULT and then saw it FORDWINE after I treated them are positively MISLEEFUL. In gratitude they've been giving me so many YELLOW-BOYS that I SCOURSED my SASHOONS for a WHITCH to carry them in. Could you please send me the design you made for a YARNWINDLE? It might be just perfect for a windmill! What do you think?

LUNG AND GAS PROBLEMS/ TWO-PECK MEASURE/ MIXTURE OF DRIED EARTH-WORMS, SAP, AND HERBS/VAT FOR SALTING MEATS/TRICK/ MARSHY GROUND/SORES/ URINE-TESTER FOR ILLS/DEATH/ FACE/FADE AWAY/INCREDU-LOUS/GOLD COINS/SWAPPED/ BOOTPADS/ CHEST/WOODEN CROSS FOR WIND-ING YARN INTO BALL

> Yours,
> Don Quixote

Dear Don,

I don't know how much longer I can hold on to this VIGIDITY. Everything's FORDWINING here, the crops included. I know you don't want others to suffer for your MISDEEDIES, but how can I keep believing in your MURLIMEWS? First it's GLEET for FERNTICLES; then it's LOP-LOACHES for

FRESH VEGETATION/ FADING AWAY

WRONGDOINGS/ ANTICS/SLIMY STUFF/FRECKLES/ LEECHES

LIFEBLOODS. Now it's another idea for windmills. What next? If you see a SHINICLE, you're off and running. When are you coming for me? I want to do the LUSTY-GALLANT with you! Soon! Before I wind up NOGGLING all alone in the GROPSING into that great REGORT for good!

Your Dulcinea

TICS
LIGHT IN THE DISTANCE
DANCE
WALKING HALTINGLY/ TWILIGHT/GULF

Dear King (Formerly Prince) Charming,

Nothing's the way it used to be between us anymore. I still seem to be NURTING a POPES-HEAD—but now in a lot more rooms than ever before—while you're SKEERING around, attending to your royal duties. Sometimes when you go off with your magic TALEVACE to cure FORMICA or to see some poor soul with KINGSEVIL, I go up to the SKY-PARLOR and PRAG my VULT with a FLURCH of PULPATOONS all by myself, remembering your foot rubs and watching for your return in the TIMWHISKY—which you never take me for a ride in these days. Maybe I'm just too UNPREGNANT to be queen. I can't help it if some ABACTOR stole your prize bulls. And if I have to spend one more afternoon entertaining BEDLAWYERS, or need to present even one more MACKALLOW, or excuse myself when I WEMBLE at a TUTTING, I shall FREAM! As for continuing the royal line, I'm sick and tired of BEDGANG. I've TIDDERED enough with you already. You FOADED me with that FABURDEN royal line of "Happily ever after," and it really can't TURKESS for me than this. Please go do your PICKTHANKING number on some SEEKSORROW. I've had it!

Cinderella

PUSHING/ BROOM WITH LONG HANDLE TO REACH HIGH PLACES/RACING

SHIELD/DISEASE IN HAWKS/ ULCERATED GLANDS CURED BY KING'S TOUCH/ ATTIC/STUFF/ FACE/BUNCH/ DELICACIES/ CARRIAGE DRAWN BY ONE OR TWO HORSES/ INEPT AT BUSINESS/ CATTLE STEALER

THE BEDRIDDEN

GIFT TO FOSTER CHILD/INVERT CUP TO REFUSE TEA/WOMEN'S TEA PARTY/ SCREAM/ CONFINEMENT BEFORE BIRTH/ HAD CHILDREN/ BEGUILED/HIGH-SOUNDING/GET WORSE/ FLATTERY/ EMOTIONAL MASOCHIST

My precious Cinderella,

Guess what? I found a terrific little inn near the FAIRY-CIRCLES where they serve the best buns with KISSINGCRUSTS (no, not true, yours are still the best of all) and where we can UNPUCKER for a while in GO-SUMMER. No FAMPLING for a week or two—how does that sound? And I'm bringing home a new SARPE and a HALF-CAP that'll look so great on you. Please don't EXCARNIFICATE me like this! Give me another chance!

Yours forever,
K (FP)C

CIRCULAR PLOTS OF LAND WITH SHORT GRASS/ SIDES OF BAKED GOODS STUCK TO-GETHER IN OVEN/ RELAX/LATE FALL/FEEDING CHILDREN/GOLD NECKLACE/HEAD-DRESS WITH RIBBONS AND FLOWERS/TEAR TO PIECES

Dear Mickey,
    Squeak!
    I found a great place down at the FOUNCE of a
GREEZE here that I want to take you to see. The
ABBEY-LUBBER's been saving me leftovers of
SINGING-BREAD whenever there's been an
ARTOLATRY service. Isn't that nice?

Squeak!
Minnie

BOTTOM

FLIGHT OF STAIRS/
RETIRED FRIAR/
WAFERS USED FOR
MASS
WORSHIP OF
BREAD

Dear Minnie,
    Squeak! Squeak!
    While you've been away, I've been saving you
MANNERS-BITS of cheese. I've filled almost a whole
GOTCH! Just think: Wouldn't it be GEASON if
someday we could get out of this tiny DREAM-HOLE
and find a whole magic SUMMER-CASTLE just for the
two of us?!

Squeak!
Mickey

SCRAPS

EARTHENWARE
JUG/WONDERFUL/
SLIT IN WALL
ADMITTING
LIGHT/TOWER

Dear Stanley,

I don't care if you see me as a SORN. What I see is the way you VEY me. Don't you think a Southern belle can tell? I know those MISLOOKS of yours. I know you're sending me AMORETS, even in the way you MISHEARKEN whenever your friend comes over to visit. But it's really you and me, Stanley, who belong together. The way your undershirt GUMBLES; the way you CLOINTER up the GREEZE; the way you SLURG around the apartment and CHANK and FROAM and KELK and throw your SCORKS around—it's all music to my ears. I want to lick your HEEL-TAPS; I want you to PRANGLE me in your CLARTY bowling shirt; I want you to SOWL me on the floor from room to room. I can NURRY you better than Stella in her tacky MARRY-MUFF. Your UNSNOD, CRIZZLED hands belong on my GREADE, not hers. Go ahead; be a FULYEAR! Who cares about the AFTERCLAPS?

> Yours!
> Blanche

SPONGE
EXAMINE
SINFUL LOOKS
LOVING GLANCES
LISTEN SINFULLY

HANGS LOOSE / STOMP / STAIRS / MOVE SLUGGISHLY / EAT NOISILY / GRUNT / BELCH / APPLE CORES / DREGS LEFT IN LIQUOR BOTTLE / SQUEEZE TIGHTLY / FILTHY / PULL BY THE EARS / NOURISH / DRESS MADE OF CHEAP MATERIAL / ROUGH / SUNBURNED / BOSOM / DEFILER OF WOMEN / CONSEQUENCES

Dear Blanche,

Your BUMROLL—it makes me WALM. Me? BLENCH at you, Blanche? Hah! I'd rather CONSTUPRATE a MOLDWARP! Read the STELLISCRIPT, Blanche. It'll always be me 'n' Stella. So get your fancy FOUNCE out of my VULT by TWATTER-LIGHT, or the next FRAGOR you hear will be the FARY of some not very kind strangers, PRAGGING you and your DRYFATS into a streetcar.

> Stanley

SKIRT PADDING / NAUSEATED / GIVE SIDELONG GLANCES / RAVISH / MOLE / WRITING IN THE STARS / BOTTOM / FACE / TWILIGHT / LOUD NOISE / COMMOTION STUFFING / BOXES

55

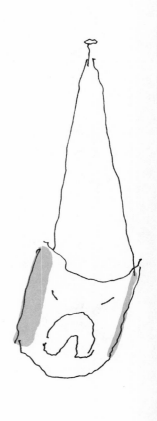

$\mathcal{M}$IXED
······
EMOTIONS

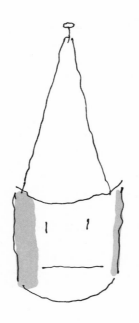

TV INTERVIEW

. . . .

HOST: Let's all welcome Dave DRICKSIE, bass
guitarist for the STIGS! Hey there, Dave,
you're looking specially SNARP tonight.

> DECAYED
>
> SHY, MODEST
>
> SHARP

DAVE: You mean this FRIED SHIRT? Hey, thanks.
My special friend got it for me, I think it was
in Amsterdam.

> STIFF-FRONTED
> SHIRT

HOST: Sure looks NIASSY with the jeans and all,
real snarp. So how's it going between you
and this woman friend of yours? The press's
been saying your relationship is, uh, sort of,
um, TEALT?

> WILD
>
> SHAKY

DAVE: Well, yeah, it's, uh, tealt all right. Kinda off
and on, but when we're together, it's real
great. Like she gets into a big FOGUE when
the papers blow stuff way outa proportion.
Like that time I hung out for a coupla hours
in the SKY-PARLOR in Chicago with the
promoter's niece. JERNIE! They make it
sound like my pants were DABBIN' DOWN
around my ankles or somethin', when all I
was doin' was PRAGGIN' time for the good of
the group. But she knows the score. We're
pretty CLOVE AND ORANGE when we're
together, no problem.

> FURIOUS FIT
>
> THEATER ATTIC
>
> A MILD OATH
>
> HANGING DOWN
> LIKE WET
> CLOTHES
>
> FILLING UP
>
> CLOSE,
> INTIMATE

HOST: You going off on another tour soon?

DAVE: Yeah, real GEASON one too. We'll be
SKEERIN' through Denmark, Norway,
Sweden, Finland, and Germany.

> WONDERFUL
>
> MOVING

HOST: How long will you be on tour then?

DAVE: 'Bout three months. And we'll get to YERR with a lotta the great new bands over there.

MAKE A LOT OF NOISE

HOST: And your girlfriend, is she going too?

DAVE: Sure, well, for part of the time. She's terrific on tour. After each GET-PENNY, the FLESHMENT's totally awesome.

PROFITABLE PERFORMANCE/ EXCITEMENT

HOST: How about an end to this WIFTHING then? Are you preparing your fans for a wedding?

PLAYING AROUND

DAVE: Hey, whoa, like not yet. We're both TARTLIN' on that. Heavy COPESMATES, yeah, but like they say, "UNPUCKER." Okay?

HESITATING

COMPANIONS

RELAX, COOL IT

PRISON INTERVIEW

. . . .

ANNOUNCER: Radio station WOWF presents another of its *Meet the Public* features with a live broadcast from the county prison. Today we're interviewing one of the "lost souls" whose crimes of passion have rendered them as lost to society as the lost words they use.

> PARTIALLY DERANGED

INT: Madam, what despicable crime was your ticket of admission here?

PRI: A crime of RAVARY, all right. VATICIDE.

> FIT OF PASSION / MURDER OF POETS

INT: Could you explain?

PRI: Vaticide. I kill poets. Like my husband.

INT: Poets? Not your typical crime, I would imagine. For what reason?

PRI: If they MISENGLISH. It's repulsive to me. So I kill 'em.

> MISUSE LANGUAGE BY MISQUOTING OR TRANSLATING INCORRECTLY

INT: What exactly did your husband do that was so offensive?

PRI: Well, for years he promised to stop using words that didn't fit his meaning. But he didn't. It became an obsession with 'im. A surefire way to get at me. Some poet. Became as abusive as all those profit seekers and plagiarists and people who withhold COPY-MONEY. A little voice up here tells me to EXCARNIFICATE 'em all.

> MONEY OWED FOR MANUSCRIPT / TEAR TO PIECES

INT: How would you do it?

PRI: I used to be a critic. I'd SMOOR 'em with bad *[SMOOR: SMOTHER]* press. I'd make 'em FORDWINE right before *[FORDWINE: FADE AWAY]* your eyes.

INT: Very crafty.

PRI: Yes, I like it. Very clean. No ACHARNE. *[ACHARNE: BLOODTHIRSTY FURY]*

INT: Well, now that you're here, do you help other prisoners as a means to getting out yourself?

PRI: I've been helping that JACKMAN over there. He wants to become a COUPLE-BEGGAR, so I've been showing 'im how to write marriage certificates.
[JACKMAN: EDUCATED BEGGAR/PERSON; COUPLE-BEGGAR: IN BUSINESS TO MARRY BEGGARS TO EACH OTHER]

INT: That sounds commendable.

PRI: Thank you.

INT: Do you have a roommate?

PRI: Yes, but she's getting out in a week. Been here just a year, since all she did was just DELUMBATE her sister's new FRANION, no big deal. Got her sentence reduced for being WOWF. But she's so SNARP. While she's been working in the prison lab, she discovered a lot of great new uses for THARM—like for tying up YELMS, and for dental floss, and to get out earwax.
[DELUMBATE: EMASCULATE/FRANION: HEARTTHROB; WOWF: PARTIALLY DERANGED/SNARP: SHARP/THARM: TWISTED INTESTINES/YELMS: STRAW BUNDLES]

INT: Now wait a minute! Wouldn't most people call what she did a real ravary, rather than what you did?

PRI: Maybe, but most of us in here don't think like other people. We go by our own rules. Like a FLITWITE means nothing to us, but whoever's guilty of ASSART—there's a real crime! He should be made to swing on a FORCHE overlooking his own wasteland.

FINE FOR BRAWLING / DEFORESTING LAND / FORK-SHAPED GALLOWS

INT: You mean you care about things like the environment, like trees and stuff?

PRI: Absolutely! This COSMOTECTURE needs a lot of protection. Animals too. Take that guy, Lyndonne, over there. He SOWLED his dog. No one should get away with that. Especially since the dog was in LOVESHIP at the time. That's a real ravary for you.

THIN OUTER LAYER OF THE WORLD PULLED BY THE EARS

ACT OF MAKING LOVE

INT: I see. And can you tell me about that man there in the robe?

PRI: He's our resident SEEKSORROW. Pretends he's a priest. He gets out and comes right back in again for the same ravary, CHOP-CHURCH. And see that SMICKLY-looking guy over there? With the golf clubs? He's the newest. Gonna be here a long time.

MASOCHIST

CHARGING MONEY FOR RELIGIOUS FAVORS / SMART

INT: Golf clubs?

PRI: Probably'll be SWEEKING those till his FORTHFARE. Bought 'em with his greed. Made a pile real fast pocketing RADDLINGS. Finally got caught cheating PUTTERS-OUT. We're gonna check 'im out tonight. Give 'im a big CHUMMING-UP and see what he pays. Some of the guys've been TOOTLING for days. 'Scuse me.

SWINGING / DEATH / ELECTION BRIBERY MONEY / INVESTORS IN HIGH-RISK LOANS / "WELCOME" TO NEW PRISONER WITH BRIBES

SINGING NOTES UNDER BREATH

I've got to go and rehearse. . . . "For he's a
jolly good . . ."

INT: That's how it goes, folks. Seems like one man's
ravary is just another's HURKLE. Right?   SHRUG OF
                                                 SHOULDERS

. . . .

*M*y dear First Lady-to-be, first let me thank you for giving up your NOONSCAPE so that I might share my vision of FRITH with you. I have a SWEVEN. And in that sweven I am reading the STELLISCRIPT through the COSMOTECTURE. It tells of a STILLWORTH era that you and I, together as a team, can usher in for our great nation.

We both love our wonderful country. We both QUAGGLE in agony at seeing anyone who DRY-DITCHES at his labors only to be FRASKED out of his YELLOW-BOYS. "No more SLOCKSTERS! No PRESSGANGS!" I say. With you at my side I can hope to rid our land of VAFROUS ABBEY-LUBBERS and SORNING AXWADDLERS!

Have you not also seen how many more STEWED PRUNES there are now than ever before? Signs are everywhere that the previous administration let our nation WROX. They allowed FOGORNERS to CUDDY our people. They are responsible for the AVERINGS in our alleys and the URFS in our streets. Let us strike a YACK against this HOGO! A nation UNSNOD and UNPREGNANT cannot prevail!

We can make it all work again, my dear HALF-MARROW. I see us bringing together a nation of MEAT-GIVERS, generous to HALF-STRAINERS, in which THUFTENS can FAMPLE their BOUFFAGE after an honest day of DRESSER KNOCKING.

Margin glosses:

NOONSCAPE — LUNCHTIME

FRITH — PEACE

SWEVEN — DREAM

STELLISCRIPT / COSMOTECTURE / STILLWORTH — WRITING IN THE STARS / THIN OUTER LAYER OF THE WORLD / PEACEFUL

QUAGGLE / DRY-DITCHES / FRASKED / YELLOW-BOYS / SLOCKSTERS / PRESSGANGS / VAFROUS / ABBEY-LUBBERS / SORNING / AXWADDLERS — SHAKE LIKE JELLY / WORKS FRUITLESSLY / TRICKED / GOLD COINS / SERVANT ROBBERS / STREET GANGS / CUNNING / FAKE FRIARS / SPONGING / ABSENTEES FROM COMBAT / FRUIT (DEEMED CURATIVE) ON WINDOWSILLS AS SIGN OF BROTHEL

WROX / FOGORNERS / CUDDY / AVERINGS / URFS — DECAY / EVICTORS / BRIBE / NAKED BEGGAR BOYS / URCHINS

YACK / HOGO / UNSNOD / UNPREGNANT — BLOW / STENCH / IN DISORDER / INEPT AT BUSINESS / WIFE

MEAT-GIVERS / HALF-STRAINERS / THUFTENS / FAMPLE / BOUFFAGE / DRESSER KNOCKING — HOSPITABLE PEOPLE / MIDDLE-CLASS STRIVERS / MAIDS / FEED CHILDREN / COMPLETE DINNERS / ANNOUNCING MEALS

And if we encounter ABLUDERS, we will listen to their TARTLING and invite them to turn their TIFLING into positive thinking. Previous leaders may have FOADED innocent people with their DOUBLE-TONGUES but not us. We will lead our citizens out of their DREAM-HOLES to action! To becoming POT-WABBLERS! To ask not what their FOLKMOTES can do for them, but what they can do for their folkmotes!

It is true, my First Mate, though we may wish it otherwise, that none of this can be done WITH A WET FINGER. Any DUMB-WIFE (pardon, my dear) knows that. It will take time. And during our time

DISSENTERS

SKEPTICISM

FOMENTING OF TROUBLE/ DECEIVED/ DUPLICITY

WALL SLITS ADMITTING LIGHT/ BOROUGH ACTIVISTS/ VILLAGE ASSEMBLIES

EASILY/ FORTUNE-TELLER

in office we will offer SAY-WELLS rather than KELK over past TURKESSES. We will implement programs to reward good deeds. Like FORFANG. And reconvene local MORN-SPEECHES. PROFACES to everyone who'll become a WHIFFLER and FRITHBURGHER for us all!

And now I ask you, my dearest partner, to consider our own BABIES-IN-THE-EYES. Look closely into my eyes. Do you not see the same sweven as your own? My sweven is your sweven—for a future of VIGIDITY for the two of us and for our great country. I am so proud to have you by my side. Forgive me if my words seem WANMOL or wanting; my FLESHMENT is not.

Come with me to the window. See how the UNDER-BRIGHT is shining through? Let us go forward together, SOLIDUNGULOUS and FRIM, as we greet the GRAKING of a better tomorrow!

COMPLIMENTS/ GROAN/TURNS FOR WORSE

RESCUING STOLEN GOODS/ GUILD MEETINGS/ HEARTY SALUTES/ PARADE LEADER/ GUARDIAN OF PEACE

REFLECTION OF ONESELF IN ANOTHER'S PUPILS

FLOURISHING GROWTH

CLUMSY

INTENSE EXCITEMENT

LIGHT BENEATH CLOUDS/COMPLETE, WHOLE-HOOFED/ BOLD/EARLY DAWN

I, MEVERLY MELSH-DICK, being of SOLIDUNGULOUS mind, declare this to be my last will and testament, as follows:

1. I direct that all my debts against my estate and the expenses for my FORTHFARE, including those for a PARCEL-GILT WHITCH, be paid as FOOT-HOT as possible.

2. I appoint as executors and trustees the firm of SNIRP, SNARP & SNOOL, and empower these principals with the STILLWORTH liquidation of my estate.

3. To my husband, GOORDY, I bequeath all the YELLOW-BOYS I have kept in secret over the years. And to him I leave this parting message as well: Our CLOVE AND ORANGE marriage since our first FLESHMENT and BRIDELOPE has given me much SEELIHEAD because of his NIASSY ideas for RAVARIES, the best being the FRAMP in the SLUT-GRATE when he FLUNGED his big WAPPER all around the SWEEK-BAR. Though I objected at first, his purchase of an extravagant CAT-BAND for our bedroom was truly prudent in discouraging children from entering as his FREAMING increased. As for the GOTCH of DRICKSIE STEWED PRUNES I discovered in his SLOPS a month ago, I remain puzzled as to why he was carrying it around, but I moved it into our POWDERING-TUB downstairs to avoid any HOGO. I leave it to him or to the community charity organization mentioned herein (see paragraph 7) to dispose of this suitably.

Marginal glosses:

MILD-MANNERED/FOREST GOBLIN/WHOLLY SECURE

FUNERAL

PARTIALLY GILDED/COFFIN/QUICKLY

WITHER/SHARP/NAG
PEACEFUL

ROUND AND PLUMP

GOLD COINS

INTIMATE/INTENSE EXCITEMENT/WEDDING/HAPPINESS/WILD/FITS OF PASSION/REVEL/HEARTH GRATING/WAVED AND PLUNGED AT SAME TIME/LEADEN BALL ON STRAP/BAR IN FIREPLACE TO HOLD POTS/CHAIN TO SECURE A DOOR/RUTTING NOISES/JUG/DRIED/FRUIT KEPT IN BROTHELS AS CURATIVE/TROUSERS

VAT FOR SALTING MEAT/SMELL

4. To my first son, NURVIL, the WONDSOME, I bequeath all my SMERLES, which he always seemed to find uses for. To him I leave this parting message as well: I hope he'll emerge from his position as a SEEKSORROW, and I ask him to forgive me if his URF-like state might be due to any MISDIET on my part when he was a baby, contributing to his YOSKING as a child and his chronic WALMING as an adult. I hope he finds a way to cease SORNING off his family with that DRY-DITCHING PALINGMAN job of his, finally STOO and get his CATERCAP, and maybe do something worthwhile with his life—like even become a doctor! Then perhaps he could finally find some use for that collection of SKILFERS of ANGLE-TWATCHES he keeps in his DRYFATS and make some money treating WEEZLES (he'll need to choose a specialty) with things like AXUNGER and THARM. And if he bought some clothes that didn't GUMBLE, and practiced not NUDDLING so much but, instead, stood up straight like his brother GEASON, and learned to FRIKE a little better, then he could really get somewhere and find a nice PUNDLE to take care of him.

5. To my daughter, Betsy, the HIPPOED, I bequeath a number of items: my SARPE and SURPEACH; my PLUMPERS to STROAT that CHICHEVACHE of hers; my every gown and elegant

DWARFISH OR MISERLY PERSON/ TROUBLESOME/ OINTMENTS

EMOTIONAL MASOCHIST/ STUNTED CHILD/ IMPROPER FEEDING/ HICCUPPING; NAUSEA/ SPONGING/ FRUITLESS/ EEL-DEALER/GO FOR IT/ UNIVERSITY DEGREE

PIECES/EARTH-WORMS/ BARRELS/ TRACHEAS/ MIX OF HERBS, WORMS, AND SAP/TWISTED INTESTINES/FIT TOO LOOSELY/ STOOPING OVER/ WONDERFUL DANCE

SHORT, FAT WOMAN

SUFFERING FROM IMAGINARY AILMENTS/NECKLACE/ JEWEL ON TURBAN/ CHEEK PUFFERS/ FILL/THIN FACE

SUCKENY to replace her MARRY-MUFFS; and all my CHOPPINS. To her I leave this parting message: Even if she's UNPREGNANT, she should get off her SLURGING FOUNCE and get herself a job. God knows I tried to teach her to do something with those messy ELF-LOCKS of hers so she could learn to make other women's CRISPLES into BULL-TOURS or maybe even become a TIRE-WOMAN, turning their FEAKS into DORLOTS. It's time she stopped CHUNTERING about whose fault it is that she has those HURKLING IRPS of hers, put on some SMICKLY outfits, and found herself a decent HALF-MARROW. And since "the way to a man is through his HEART-SPOON," she might learn how to use good RAW-HEAD for the best FLAMMICKS ever.

6. To my second son, Geason, the SNOUT-FAIR, I bequeath as many BUNGDOWNS as it takes for him to become the FRIM DOUBLE READER he's already studying to be and to keep him outfitted in the SMOOTH-BOOTED FRIED SHIRTS, power VAMPERS, and WRAP-RASCALS befitting his profession. To him I leave this parting message: There's no profit these days in a practice chasing after COPY-MONEY. He'd do better devoting that gorgeous FABURDEN of his to prosecuting cases on more VAFROUS, lucrative issues, like STILLICIDE, VATICIDE, and ASSART. But, an UTTER-WART: "Neither a QUESTMONGER nor a FOGORNER be." I only hope he'll give up that TUMBESTER with the big GREADE and find a woman more worthy of him to SNOOZLE with in that fancy apartment of his before it's too late.

Marginal glosses:

SMOCK/CHEAP GARMENTS/HIGH-HEELED SHOES/INEPT AT BUSINESS/SLUGGISHLY MOVING/BOTTOM/TANGLED HAIR/CURLS/MASSES OF FRIZZED HAIR ON FOREHEAD/MAKER OF HEADDRESSES/CURLS/JEWELED KNOTS OF HAIR WORN ON FOREHEAD/MUTTERING/BODY-CONTRACTING/TICS/SMART-LOOKING/HUSBAND/STOMACH/CREAM THAT RISES TO TOP OF RAW MILK

DESSERTS

HANDSOME

COPPER COINS

FLOURISHING/LAWYER

FLATTERING/STIFF-FRONTED SHIRTS/SOCKS/RAKISH, LOOSE OVERCOATS

MONEY OWED FOR MANUSCRIPT/HIGH-SOUNDING, EAR-FILLING TONE/CRAFTY/DRIPPING WATER/MURDER OF POETS/DEFORESTING LAND/WARNING/LAWSUIT AGITATOR/EVICTING LANDLORD/FEMALE TUMBLER/BOSOM/SETTLE DOWN

7. Charity Donations:

To the GLOX and WROX Club Against HALF-STRAINERS, of which I've been a member for thirty years, a set of twelve cups and saucers for TUTTINGS, ten hand-PURFLED, stuffed BANKERS, and, for permanent display, the engraved CLAPDISH the club awarded me for my service to the community. To the Home for WOWF WHIFFLERS, the disposition of the aforementioned dricksie stewed prunes if my husband agrees (see paragraph 3) and the use of my SKY-PARLOR once a month to FAMPLE their AVERINGS and to amuse them with my children's old BULL-BEGGARS and SCATCHES.

In witness, I have set my hand to this will and hereby provide my signature:

Meverly Melsh-dick

SOUND OF LIQUID IN BARREL/ DECAY/MIDDLE-CLASS STRIVERS/ WOMEN'S TEA PARTIES/ EMBROIDERED/ CUSHIONS/ALMS-COLLECTING CONTAINER/ DERANGED/ OFFICERS IN PARADE

ATTIC/PUT FOOD INTO CHILD'S MOUTH/NAKED BEGGAR BOYS/ SCARY COS-TUMES/STILTS

*T*his is hardly the end. Now it's your turn to *snoozle* with as many of these lost and lovely *pulpatoons* as endear themselves to you, or lack of attention will send them back under the blanket of oblivion. Drop a few into your conversations with *copesmates*—just to see what happens.

Wherever possible—as determined by the limited availability of precise sources on words that either no longer exist or are designated "rare," "obsolete," or "dialect" in the references consulted—dates are given for the approximate time when the word was in use or is cited in the sources. For further study, except for (OED) *Oxford English Dictionary,* the name after each entry refers to the author or the editor listed in the bibliography of the work in which the word is mentioned.

*A*BACTOR A person who drove away or stole cattle in herds or in large numbers at a time; 1650s–1800s. (OED)

ABBEY-LUBBER A slothful loiterer in a house of religion, pretending to be retired yet dedicated to his religion. Dryden employed a similar term, *sucking friar.* (McAdam)

ABLUDE To differ, disagree, be out of keeping with, be unharmonious, literally out of tune, from Latin *ab* "away from" and *ludere* "to play an instrument"; 1600s. (OED)

ACHARNE To thirst for blood, in the 1400s to give a taste of flesh to dogs and falcons, from Latin *carnem* "flesh"; n. English military term for bloodthirsty fury, ferocity; 1800s. (OED)

AFTERCLAP An unexpected consequence, usually unpleasant; 1420–1860s. (OED, Skeat)

AIMCRIER An adviser, applauder, encourager, the person who cried "Aim!" to encourage an archer, the one who stood near the target to report results of each round; 1600–1700s. (OED)

AMORET A loving look or glance; 1500–1600s. (Skeat)

ANGLE-TWATCH. Also *angle-twitch, angel-touche.* An earthworm, from French *anguille,* derived from Old English *angul* "to bend" and *twicce* "twitch, pierce with a nail"; believed to be cure for sickness when ground into solution of oil and vinegar and drunk cold three times a day; 900–1700s. (OED, Nares)

ARTOLATRY The worship of bread, resulting from confusing the meaning of the Eucharist with the ritual itself; 1610–1658. (OED)

ASSART The crime of yanking up trees by the roots for plowing, thereby turning forests into plains; *assart-rent*—1670s legal term for fee paid to the Crown for forest land cleared by permission; 1200–1800s. (OED, McAdam)

ASS-RIDDLIN The custom in Yorkshire once a year when ashes were *riddled* (sifted) on the hearth in belief that if any member of the family were to die within that year, the shape of that person's shoes would appear in the ashes. (Halliwell)

AVERING A young boy who pretended to be cold and destitute by stripping off clothes and begging in town to gain sympathy and better clothing. (Wright)

AXUNGER Soft, fat grease mixed with powdered earthworms, tree sap, and herbs to make a plaster for open wounds, from Latin *axungia* "greasy matter"; *axunge* still applies to rich fat of geese and pig kidneys. (OED, Wright)

AXWADDLE Also *askefise*. A coward who stayed home by the fire while others went to combat and who became dirty with ashes from being so lazy, from Swedish *aske* "ashes" and *fisa* "blow, pass wind"; 1300–1500s. (Shipley)

ℬABIES-IN-THE-EYES The reflection of oneself in another person's pupils; a popular pastime in days before mirrors was "to look babies." (Halliwell)

BANKER A cushion or chair pillow, from Saxon *banc* "hill, elevated ground"; 1300–1600s. (Toone)

BATTERFANGED Verbally beaten as though clawed; 1630–1800s. (Nares)

BEAU-TRAP Loose pavement in footpath under which dirt and water collected, causing splashing when stepped upon. (Halliwell)

BEDGANG Lying in, confinement to bed. (Mackay)

BEDLAWYER A bedridden person, 1440; term became *bedlar* by 1860. (Halliwell)

BELLY-FRIEND An insincere person interested in others only to take advantage for his own purposes. (Halliwell)

BESPAWLED Spattered with saliva; 1600s. (OED)

BLENCH A side-glance, a glimpse, related to *blink*; led to idea of playing a trick, cheating. (OED)

BLETCH Black soot, dirt, ink, or matter that adhered to wheel axles. (OED, Wright)

BOUFFAGE A satisfying meal eaten so greedily that filled-up mouth made cheeks swell, from French *bouffer* "to swell"; 1672. (Skeat)

BRIDELOPE A wedding, from Old Teutonic *brudi* "bride" and *hlaup* "run or leap," yielding "bridal run," the gallop of the new bridegroom conducting his bride to their new home, cited in the *Lindisfarne Gospels* in 950; became *broose* in northern countryside of Britain and Scotland, where all men from wedding party took part in a race by horse or on foot from wedding chapel to new couple's house; "to ride the broose" meant to be awarded colored silk handkerchief as the prize of contest held in 1700s and 1800s (see introduction). (OED, Shipley)

BRINCH To drink, to toast, from Italian *brinsi* "I drink to you"; 1500s. (OED, Halliwell)

BROWNSWINE A porpoise; 1440. (OED)

BRUSTLE A crackling sound; a swishing noise like that of waves of the sea; 1200–1750. (OED, Skeat)

BUBUKLE A red or inflamed pimple on face, from combination of *bubo* "a sore" and *carbuncle*; 1600s. (OED, Toone)

BUGLE-BEARD A shaggy beard like buffalo hair. (Davies)

BULL-BEGGAR An object designed to scare a person; a sacklike garment with openings for eyes and arms put on by person assigned to whip an apprentice, from Welsh *bwg* "ghost," and Scottish *bogle* "goblin," which was altered to become *boggard*, then *beggar*; 1500–1850. (OED)

BULL-TOUR A mass of frizzy hair worn by woman on forehead, from French *taure* "bull"; also known as a *frowse*; 1690–1700s. (OED)

BUMROLL A bustle, or padding under woman's skirt over hip area; also called *bumrowl* and *bum-barrel*. (Shipley)

BUNGDOWN A large copper coin used in Aroostook County, Maine, from *bungtown* "a copper counterfeit English penny"; 1909–1934. (Wentworth)

𝒞ARE-CLOTH A canopy held over or placed on heads of bride and groom during marriage service, possibly from French *carré* "square," or from *cark* "worry" (see following); also called *carke-cloth*; in use since Anglo-Saxon times to acknowledge higher powers in a gesture of respect, humility, and prayer, while asking for blessing and future protection; used metaphorically in 1624 work "A Care-Cloth, or a Treatise of the Cumbers and Troubles of Matrimony"; through 1800s (see introduction). (OED)

CARKED Fretfully anxious (see previous); 1400–1800s. (OED, Mackay)

CAT-BAND A bar or iron chain to secure a door or to defend a street, found to be insufficient for prisons; 1600s. (OED)

CATERCAP A square cap worn by university graduates and academics, came to mean university man himself, from French *quatre* "four," referring to four corners of dice or of cards that fit together to form shape of four-cornered top of cap; led to *catty-corner* "in a diagonal or oblique position"; late 1500s–1600s. (OED)

CHANK To eat noisily, chomp; 1500s–1600s. (Skeat)

CHICHEVACHE (term of insult) A thin, ugly face, from French *chinchefache* "ugly, thin face," which English adopted as *-vache*, meaning "lean cow"; became proper name for fabled monster in 1300–1400s who fed only on patient wives, the scarcity of which kept him lean and hungry. (OED)

CHOP-CHURCH A dealer or secular "priest" who traded blessings, religious favors, and reassurances of grace for payment; 1300s–1700. (OED)

CHOPPINS High-heeled shoes, from Spanish *chapin* "a high, cork shoe"; 1550–1700s. (Skeat, Davies)

CHUMMING-UP The practice of prisoners' brandishing swords and weapons as a "welcome" to a new inmate in expectation of his paying money as "price of admission" to their company, also termed *garnish*; 1700s. (Halliwell)

CHUNTER To complain, grumble, mutter; 1600–1800s. (OED, Halliwell)

CLAMBERSCULL Very strong ale. (Halliwell)

CLAPDISH A wooden dish for collecting alms, having a cover that shut with a sharp, clapping sound, and used by beggars to get attention; term also for a talkative person; 1500s–1800s. (OED, Skeat)

CLAPPERCLAW To scold, "beat" with one's tongue; n. a scold; 1500s–1800s. (McAdam)

CLART A chunk of hardened mud or dirt; led to insulting term *clarty-paps*, a messy, slovenly wife; 1800s. (Halliwell)

CLOINTER To tread heavily. (Mackay)

CLOVE AND ORANGE A term for intimacy, close relationship, from custom of sticking oranges with cloves, roasting them, and using as ingredients in a brewed liquor named *bishop*. (Toone)

CONSTUPRATE To rape, defile, violate, from Latin *stuprum* "ravishing, defiling"; 1550–1600s. (OED)

COPESMATE A companion, friend. (McAdam)

COPY-MONEY The sum paid to an author for his manuscript or for copyright, from *copy* "property or one's right of ownership"; 1700–1800s. (OED)

COSMOTECTURE A figurative thin lining around the world; 1600s. (OED)

COUPLE-BEGGAR A person in business to marry beggars to each other. (McAdam)

COURT HOLY WATER To flatter, use fancy words without deeds; 1550–1700. (Skeat)

CRISPLE A tiny curl, tendril; 1600s. (Mackay)

CRIZZLE A rough, sunburned area on face or hand, from French *crisser* "to crackle"; 1800s. (OED)

CUDDY A bribe, from Irish *cuid oidliche* "evening portion," the supper and light entertainment a tenant felt obliged to "pay" to his lord, which later became an outright gift or rent; 1450–1800s. (OED)

CURTAIN-SERMON A reproof given by wife to husband at bedtime; 1600s on (see introduction). (OED)

CYMBAL-DOCTOR An ineffective teacher, like an instrument that makes a loud but empty sound. (Davies)

*D*ABBING-DOWN Hanging down like wet clothes. (Skeat)

DEAD-LIFT (AT DEAD LIFT) A last extremity, hopeless point of desperation, from the use of a horse to pull or move something of dead weight; 1500s–1800s. (OED, Nares)

DELUMBATE To maim (either sex), emasculate, from Latin *lumbus* "loin, flank"; 1600s. (Halliwell)

DENTISCALP A toothpick, from Latin *dens* "tooth" and *scalpere* "to scratch"; 1600s–1800s. (OED, Shipley)

DEVILSHINE Demonic power or skill; 1050–1300. (OED)

DILLIGROUT A type of stew or soup offered to British kings by lords of manors in return for their position; 1662–1880. (OED)

DORLOT A woman's headdress in the form of a knot of hair arranged on her forehead with a jewel added; 1340–1440. (OED)

DOUBLE READER A lawyer in his second course of studies after seven years in first. (McAdam, Skeat)

DOUBLE-TONGUE Duplicity, insincerity in speech; deceitful person; 1386–1850. (OED)

DREAM-HOLE An opening left in walls of barns, towers, and steeples to allow light and sound to pass through; 1600s–1800s. (OED, Halliwell)

DRESSER KNOCKING The custom in which a cook knocked on dresser to inform servants that dinner was ready to be brought to dining hall. (Toone)

DRETCH To torment, especially in one's sleep; 900–1500. (OED)

DRICKSIE Decayed, such as old timber. (Skeat)

DRY-DITCH To labor in vain, getting no results. (Davies)

DRYFAT A large box, cask, or barrel for holding dry items; 1526–1600s. (OED, McAdam)

DUMB-WIFE A fortune-teller, from idea that person without speech might have power to see the future (see introduction). (Halliwell)

*E*ARTHAPPLE A cucumber; 1000. (OED)

ELF-LOCKS Tangled hair; 1500s on. (Halliwell)

ENTERBATHE To intermingle tears; to bathe together. (Davies)

EVEGLOM Twilight; 1900s. (Wentworth)

EXCARNIFICATE To torment, torture, from Latin *carnifex* "executioner" and *excarnificare* "to tear to pieces"; 1563–1611. (OED)

EYEBITE To bewitch with the eye; 1584–1800. (OED)

EYE-WAITER A servant who was careful only while his master was watching him. (Davies)

*F*ABURDEN A high tone or noise that filled the ear or resounded loudly. (Halliwell)

FAIRHEAD Beauty; 1250–1560. (OED)

FAIRY-CIRCLES Green circles visible on short grass, supposedly made by dancing fairies but actually by fungus. (Nares)

FAMPLE To put food into a child's mouth; 1230. (OED)

FARDRY The action of painting the face white for cosmetic improvement; 1430. (OED)

FARLIES Wonders, strange sights, from Old English *faerlic* "sudden, unexpected" and Middle English *ferly* "strange, wonderful." (Skeat)

FARY A state of tumult, commotion, consternation; 1500s. (OED, Halliwell)

FATILOQUIST A fortune-teller, one who spoke fate; 1650–1700s. (OED)

FEAK A curl, from seventeenth-century term *feague* "to whip"; also from sixteenth-century term *bumfeague* "to spank"; falconry term from fifteenth to nineteenth centuries meaning "to wipe after feeding," from German *fegen* "cleanse"; also to fidget, busy oneself with trifles; 1500s–1800s. (Shipley)

FERNTICLE A freckle or mark on skin resembling seed of fern, from Scottish *fairntickle*; defined in an 1876 glossary as "the brown pin-point pops clustered in the complexion"; 1483–1800s. (OED)

FLABERKIN Puffed out, puffy, from Latin *flare* "to blow." (OED)

FLAMMICK A confection made with butter, eggs, and cheese; 1600. (OED)

FLESHMENT Excitement from a first success at an endeavor, arousal from being inflamed, from *flesh* "to give a hawk a taste of flesh from the first game killed so as to excite it to hunt further"; also to initiate or harden a person to warfare; 1500s–1600s. (Shipley)

FLESH-SHAMBLES A place where animals were killed or sold for food, a slaughterhouse; also a brothel; 1400–1600. (OED)

FLESH-SPADE A fingernail. (Davies)

FLITWITE A fine for brawling, from Old English *flitan* "to be eager, show zeal," and Scottish *witan* "to blame"; 1300–1600s. (OED)

FLODDER To blubber, disfigure the face by weeping; 1513. (OED)

FLOIT To whistle. (Toone)

FLUNGE To fly and plunge at the same time, fling out suddenly; 1500s. (OED)

FLURCH A multitude of things, not of persons; 1751. (Shipley)

FLURN To sneer at, scorn, spurn, show contempt; still in dialect use; 1650s–1860s. (OED)

FOAD To lead a person on, beguile with kind words, give excuses in order to gain time; 1300s–1600s. (OED, Skeat)

FOGORNER A person who expelled people from their buildings. (Halliwell)

FOGUE Fury, ardor, passion, from Italian *foga* "violent force"; 1600s. (Skeat)

FOLKMOTE A meeting, a town assembly, from *moot* "hill, the place to meet to resolve questions"; 1000–1800s. (Toone)

FOODER A cask to hold up to forty gallons of wine; 1679–1800. (OED)

FOOT-CLOTH A large, richly ornamented cloth of velvet with gold laid over horse's back, hanging down to ground on each side, a sign of dignity and importance; 1480–1800s. (OED)

FOOT-HOT Hastily, following close-by; 1300–1600. (OED)

FORCHE The gallows, from Old French *forche* "fork-shaped, divided"; 1380–1584. (OED)

FORDWINE To vanish, fade away, from Middle Dutch *verdwijnen* "to wither, decay"; 1000–1400. (OED)

FOREBROADS The milk from cows right after calving, same as colostrum, which could cause disease; 1800s. (OED)

FORFANG According to Old English law around the year 1000, the rescuing of stolen property and a reward for same; by 1250 a fine for taking provisions from a market before royal purveyors were served, from *feng* "capture." (OED)

FORMICA A disease in hawks; abscess or ulcer oozing from hawk's bill; 1400s–1600s; sore in dog's ear; 1800s. (Halliwell)

FORTHFARE Death; a funeral; the bell rung to signify a person's death; 800–1540. (OED)

FOUNCE The bottom, from Latin *fundus* "bottom"; 1300–1500. (OED)

FRAGOR A loud crash or noise, from Latin *frangere* "to break"; 1600–1700s. (Toone)

FRAMP, FRAMPLE n. and v. Frolic, revel, indulge in greedily; 1532. (OED)

FRANION A reckless, devil-may-care fellow who wooed many women; 1570–1800s. (OED)

FRASK A trick; 1500s. (OED)

FREAM A growl, grunt, roar, shouting, screaming, often applied to noise made by a boar at rutting time; 1500s–1700s. (OED, Davies)

FRIED SHIRT A shirt with a stiff front, from West Indian dialect; 1900s. (Wentworth)

FRIKE Lusty, vigorous, strong, joyful; v. to dance, move briskly; 1000–1475. (OED)

FRIM Flourishing, fleshy, juicy, vigorous, from Old English *freme* "forward, bold, advancing"; 1000–1888 (see introduction). (OED)

FRITH Peace, protection, safety, security, from Old Teutonic *fri* "to love," the root of *friend*; from 1500–1800s a *frithburgher* was a "keeper of the peace," a "protector" of townfolk; around the year 1000 the *frith-stool* was a place of safety and refuge in the form of a stone seat near the church altar where one could find total protection, later called the "chair of peace" or "freed stool." (OED)

FRUNDEL A dry measure equal to two pecks, used for malt, barley; 1550–1700. (OED)

FUCUS Rouge made from rock lichen that produced a red dye; 1550–1855. (OED)

FULYEAR A person who dishonored women, from *foil* "to foul, trample upon"; 1500s. (OED)

GANDERMOONER A man who chased women during the month after his wife had a child; in remote parts of Britain *gander-moon* still means the month of a wife's recovery. (Skeat)

GARBAGER An officer in the royal kitchen in charge of poultry, from verb *to garbage* "to disembowel or to gut fish"; 1600s. (OED)

GARBOIL Turmoil, commotion, hubbub; 1500s–1800s. (Mackay)

GEASON Wonderful, rare, uncommon; 1550–1700s. (Toone)

GET-PENNY A theater term for a very profitable performance. (Nares)

GLEEKMAN A professional entertainer at a social gathering or a musician, from Saxon *gligman* "a droll, a mimic"; led to *glee* "the enhanced state of mind produced by music"; 897–1500s. (Mackay)

GLEET Sticky, greasy matter; discharge from sores; ulcerated blemish; from Old French *glette* "slimy material like the white of an egg"; 1400s–1800s. (OED)

GLOX The sound of liquids when shaken in a barrel. (Halliwell)

GOOD-HOUR The "favorable" time when a woman is in labor. (Halliwell)

GOORDY Plump, round. (Wright)

GO-SUMMER The summerlike period in late autumn, from Middle English *gosesomere* "goose" plus "summer," or "goose-summer," the time when geese were in season; also German *Gansemonat*, the "geese-month" of November; time when people in Scotland noticed filmy substance like spider webs floating in the warmer air above grass and named it *go-summer* for the time of year when it appeared; became *gossamer*, and was later applied to gauzelike materials; 1500–1800 (see introduction). (OED)

GOTCH An earthenware jug with big belly; term also applied to very round person; 1500s–1600s. (Shipley)

GOUND Sticky matter, especially secretions as from the eye; oozing sore; 1000–1670. (OED)

GRAKING Early dawn; 1200s. (Shipley)

GRANDGORE An infectious disease that was sexually transmitted; 1400s–1600s. (OED)

GREADE A lap, bosom; 897–1300s. (OED)

GREEP A bunch; v. to clutch at, grope for. (Halliwell)

GREEZE A flight of steps, shortened from *degrees*. (McAdam)

GRIBBLE A shoot from a tree, a small branch. (Halliwell)

GROPSING Twilight; also *grasp*, *grisping*, perhaps from idea that one cannot fully grasp the fleeting time that was neither day nor night; 1600s. (OED)

GRUBBLE To feel in the dark; 1500s–1700s. (McAdam)

GUMBLE To fit badly, be too large, as clothing might be; *gumbled* also applied to condition of eyes not easy to open in morning. (Halliwell)

*H*ALCH To embrace, hold on tightly while in a person's arms; to throw arms around a person; 1300s–1600s. (OED)

HALF-CAP A woman's circular headband, trimmed with ribbons and flowers at the sides and over ears, worn in 1800s; this is related to earlier term for half-courteous salute, a minimal nod or movement of one's cap, from 1600s. (OED)

HALF-MARROW A spouse, husband or wife, perhaps from Old Norse *marg-r* "friendly, communicative"; later a partner in general; 1600s–1800s. (OED)

HALF-STRAINER A person in the middle class who strove for respectability by trying to live above his station; applied also to U.S. Southerner who did "violence to the mother tongue"; 1800s–early 1900s. (Wentworth)

HAMESUCKEN The crime of assaulting a person in his own home, then the penalty for same, later the protection from this crime, from Old English and Scottish law; 1000–1800s. (OED)

HEART-SPOON The indentation at the bottom of the breastbone, the pit of the stomach, the midriff, the navel. (Onions)

HEAVY-FOOTED Pregnant; early 1900s. (Wentworth)

HEEL-TAPS The remains of liquor left at bottom of a bottle or a glass; 1700s–1800s. (Davies)

HINK To falter, from Middle Dutch *hinken* "to halt, to limp"; 1600s–1700s. (OED)

HIPPOED Suffering from an imaginary ailment, perhaps connected to pronunciation of *hypochondria*; also bluffed or deceived; early 1900s. (Wentworth)

HOGO A strong smell, stench, from French *haut-goût* "high flavor"; 1600s. (Onions)

HOLLOW-WARE Any meat not sold specifically by butchers, such as rabbits or poultry. (Halliwell)

HOTCH To shake, be restless, move jerkily, maneuver awkwardly through a crowd. (Halliwell)

HOWDY-WIFE A midwife, perhaps from Scottish *holdie,* derived from *hold* "friendly, kind, beneficent." (Halliwell)

HURKLE A shrug of one's shoulders; a contraction of entire body in response to either pain, cold, or a cramp; 1300s–1800s. (Mackay)

INKLE To attend a party without being invited; early 1900s. (Wentworth)

IRP A contortion of the body; a grimace; 1550–1770s. (Halliwell)

JACKMAN An educated beggar who could read, write, and speak Latin and who made counterfeit licenses; 1600s–1700s. (Skeat)

JERNIE A profane oath, a swear borrowed from French *jarnidieu,* originally *"Je renie Dieu"*—"I renounce God." (Skeat)

JOLLOP The cry of a turkey. (Halliwell)

$\mathcal{K}$ELK To groan, belch. (Halliwell)

KEVVEL To walk clumsily. (Halliwell)

KIBBO-KIFT A proof of great strength or muscular power. (Halliwell)

KINGSEVIL A condition of ulcerated glands supposedly cured by the king's touch; 1600s. (McAdam)

KISSINGCRUST The place where one loaf in an oven touches another; 1600s–1700s. (McAdam)

$\mathcal{L}$AVOLT A lively dance for two people, consisting of "high and active bounds"; 1550–1660s. (Onions, Nares)

LEECH-FINGER The finger next to the little finger, with which one was advised to stir potions, the "medical finger"; from the second-century-A.D. belief held by Greeks and Romans that a delicate nerve ran from this finger directly to the heart and was thereby endowed with power like a divining rod to warn the heart if it came into contact with harmful substances; its connection to the heart led to the custom of placing a wedding band around this finger as a lifelong love link; 1000–1600s. (OED, Sperling: *Tenderfeet and Ladyfingers*)

LIB To castrate, as one did to fowl; 1600s. (Halliwell)

LIFEBLOOD A tic, involuntary quivering of the lip or eyelid. (Davies)

LIGHT-BED To ground a seagoing vessel lightly on a bed of earth; 1600s. (OED)

LOP-LOACH A leech used by surgeons to draw blood. (Halliwell)

LOVESHIP Courting; the act of making love; 1500s–1600s. (OED)

LOVET A hole left in the roof over a fireplace to let out smoke; early 1900s. (Wentworth)

LUSTY GALLANT The name of a lively dance and dance tune; 1500s. (OED)

$\mathcal{M}$ACKALLOW An item given to a foster parent when a child was transferred, for the child's reassurance and security, from Gaelic *macaladh* "fostering"; 1500s–1700s. (OED)

MALE JOURNEY A difficult day with unfortunate occurrences, from French *male journée* "evil day"; 1400s. (OED)

MALE MORTE An inflamed sore, same as *mormal* (p. 85), from French for "dead evil"; 1400s. (OED)

MALE TALENT Ill will. (Halliwell)

MALLY Foolishly fond, in keeping with Dutch saying "A mally father maketh a wicked child;" 1500s–1600s. (OED)

MAMMOTHREPT A spoiled child, from Latin term for "brought up by one's grandmother"; 1600s. (OED)

MANNERS-BIT The last piece of food left on one's plate as a propriety. (Wright)

MARRY-MUFF A cheap textile fabric or garment made from it; 1600s. (OED)

MEAT-GIVER A hospitable person; 1300–1600. (OED)

MELSH-DICK A forest goblin who protected hazelnuts from getting into hands of mischievous boys. (Halliwell)

MERRY-GALL A sore produced by chafing; 1500s. (Halliwell)

MEVERLY Bashful, mild, shy. (Wright)

MIDDLEGOOD A linen fabric of middle quality; 1500s–1600s. (OED)

MISDEEDY Doing wrong, misbehavior. (OED)

MISDELIGHT Delight in something wrong; 1300s. (OED)

MISDIET Improper feeding, unbalanced eating; 1496–1617. (OED)

MISENGLISH To translate incorrectly into English; to make up an English word illegitimately; to misquote; later n. fear of misquoting; 1560s–1700s. (OED)

MISHEARKEN To eavesdrop or listen to sinfully; 1200–1500s. (OED)

MISLEEFUL Unbelieving, incredulous, from Latin leve "belief." (OED)

MISLOOK Sinful looking; also to look unfavorably upon; 1200–1400. (OED)

MISTRESS-PIECE A "masterpiece" of feminine beauty; 1600s–1900s. (OED)

MODESTY-PIECE The narrow lace that ran along the upper part of a woman's low-cut blouse; 1700s. (McAdam)

MOLDWARP A mole, from its digging earth in and out, making rippled lines along the surface; 1500s–1600s. (Toone)

MORMAL A sore inflamed with pustules, especially on the leg, from Latin mortuum malum "dead evil"; 1600s. (OED)

MORN-SPEECH A guild meeting held the morning after a guild feast, from Dutch morgenspraak "discussion"; 1000–1400s. (OED)

MURFLE A pimple, freckle; 1600s. (Halliwell)

MURLIMEWS Foolish gestures or antics, often applied derisively to ceremonies performed by priests during blessings; 1580–1700s. (OED)

MUSKIN A sweetheart, pretty face, term of endearment for a woman; 1500s. (OED)

*N*IASSY Eccentric, odd and unexpected; 1800s–early 1900s. (Wentworth)

NOGGLE To walk awkwardly. (Mackay)

NOONSCAPE A midday break for eating and resting. (Mackay)

NUDDLE The nape of the neck; also v. to stoop when walking. (Halliwell)

NURRY To nourish, as with a child; n. a foster child, a pupil, from Old French *nurrir* "to nourish"; 1300s–1500s. (OED)

NURT To butt or push with horns; 1500s–1600s. (OED)

NURVIL A miser; a person dwarfish in size, from Icelandic *nyrfill* "a miser"; 1400s. (OED)

*P*AGGLE To bulge, hang loosely; 1550–1600s. (OED)

PALINGMAN A person who dealt in eels, from Dutch *paling* "eel"; 1480s–1860s. (OED)

PARANYMPH The best man or bridesmaid, from Greek word meaning "beside the bride"; later, a spokesperson for another, an advocate, a supporter; 1600s–1800s. (Skeat)

PARBREAK To spit up, spew, from Old English *braec* "phlegm, saliva"; 1440–1700s. (OED)

PARCEL-GILT Partially gilded, as on the inner surface of cups and silverware; 1400s–1800s. (OED)

PAWKY Sly, witty, humorous with intent to please. (Mackay)

PETER-SEE-ME A Spanish wine popular in seventeenth-century England made from grapes grown in Madeira by Pedro Ximenes, whose name became Anglicized through common use; a 1617 "Law of Drinking" toasted wines intended to treat the four humors: "I am mighty melancholy / And a quart of sack will cure me; / I am choleric as any, / Quart of claret will secure me; / I am phlegmatic as may be, / Peter-see-me must inure me; / I am sanguine for a lady, / And cool Rhenish shall conjure me." (Shipley, Halliwell)

PEW-FELLOW A person in the same situation or difficulty as another, a valuable companion; 1500s–1700s. (Toone)

PICKING-HOLE An opening in a barn wall for receiving sheaves of corn. (Halliwell)

PICKTHANK A flatterer, sycophant who curried favor; also a telltale; 1500s. (Onions)

PIMGENET A small red pimple, subject of the saying "Nine pimgenets make a pock royal." (Halliwell)

PISS-PROPHET A person who diagnosed diseases by inspecting urine; also called a *water-caster*; 1600s. (OED)

PITCHKETTLED Puzzled. (Davies)

PLUMPERS Little objects placed inside the mouth to swell out one's cheeks; 1700s. (McAdam)

POPES-HEAD A broom with a long handle for reaching ceilings and high places. (Halliwell)

POTVALIANT Heated with courage after strong drink; 1700s. (McAdam)

POT-WABBLER A person entitled to vote for members of his borough's parliament because he kept and boiled his pots in that district, thereby proving residency and sufficient means to own a separate fireplace for himself and his family; 1700–1800. (Onions, Halliwell)

POWDERING-TUB A vessel in which meat was salted; 1500s–1700s. (McAdam)

PRAG To stuff, cram, or fill to the brim; 1500s–1800s. (OED)

PRANGLE To pinch, press tightly; 1300. (OED)

PRESSGANG A band of men who roamed the streets to force people into naval service; 1700s. (McAdam)

PRESTER A burning, scorching whirlwind; 1600–1800. (OED)

PROFACE A welcoming wish of good cheer at a meal, not religious like grace; also a toast to one's health, from Italian *"Buon pro vi faccia!"*—"May it do you good!"; 1500s–1600s. (OED)

PUDDING TIME (IN PUDDING TIME) In the nick of time, from the practice of arriving just in time for dinner, since the meals of humble country folk used to begin with a pudding. (Halliwell)

PULPATOONS Delicacies, from Latin *pulpamentum* "tidbits." (Toone)

PUNDLE A short and fat woman; 1700s. (McAdam)

PURFLE To decorate or adorn, formerly with embroidery as a border; 1300s–1800s. (Shipley)

PURSICKNESS A condition of short-windedness, difficult breathing in a horse, the cure being to feed it dry figs (curative for coughs and other lung diseases); with *pursickness* in sheep, suggested cure was to change its pasture and cut its ears; condition also of internal stuffiness, producing flatulence; 1600s–1800s. (OED)

PUTTER-OUT A person who, when going abroad, deposited his money with someone who guaranteed his receiving high interest on it upon his return, the percentage of which was calculated in proportion to the danger of his trip and his chances of ever returning to claim it; 1500s–1700s. (Halliwell)

QUAGGLE To shake like jelly, quiver; early 1900s. (Wentworth)

QUATCH To betray, tell a secret. (Halliwell)

QUEACHY Wet, marshy, swampy. (Halliwell)

QUESTMONGER A starter of lawsuits or prosecutions. (McAdam)

RADDLINGS Money collected as bribe at election time. (Halliwell)

RAFF To sweep up, gather together quickly; also huddle. (McAdam)

RAVARY A violent, mad fit of passion, accompanied by a lot of noise. (Wright)

RAW-HEAD The cream that rose to the surface of raw milk or milk not yet heated. (Halliwell)

REARING-FEAST A celebratory supper held for workmen when a roof was raised, or reared, on a house. (Halliwell)

RED-GOWN A skin eruption of rosy hue common to babies within a few days of birth, originally termed *reed gounde*. (Halliwell)

REEZED Scorched, fried. (Davies)

REGORT A deep place in the sea, a gulf; 1477. (OED)

RUSH RING To "wed" without a wedding ring, a ploy to convince innocent females that the marriage was legal even without a ceremony, finally prohibited by Bishop of Salisbury in 1217; 1500s. (OED)

SANN To argue, from Old Norse *sanna* "to affirm as true"; 1200. (OED)

SARPE An elegant neck-ring of gold or silver; 1400s. (OED)

SASHOON A stuffed leather pad worn inside the leg of a boot to ease pressure, corruption of French *chausson*; 1680–1800s. (OED)

SAUCE-FLEME Swelling of the face due to inflammation caused by imbalance of salt in the body, a cure for which was applications of cucumber; 1390–1600s. (OED)

SAY-WELL Verbal approval, a compliment, qualified by the common saying "Say-well is good, but do-well is better"; 1360–1800s. (OED)

SCATCHES Stilts put on when walking in dirty places. (McAdam)

SCORK An apple core. (Wright)

SCOURSE To swap, make an exchange. (McAdam)

SEEKSORROW An emotional masochist, a person who found ways to make himself unhappy or dissatisfied. (McAdam)

SEELIHEAD Happiness, innocence, the state of being blessed by God, from Old English *saelig* "blissful, innocent, blessed, deserving of compassion"; root of *silly*, which until 1600s meant innocent, but which took on different meaning as *innocent* took on connotation of helpless. (OED)

SHAB OUT To sneak away so as to avoid an encounter or humiliation; early 1900s. (Wentworth)

SHINICLE A distant fire or bonfire, a little light seen far ahead. (Mackay)

SINGING BREAD The wafer used in celebration of the Mass, later a gift for singers at holiday time in Scotland; 1400–1800s. (OED)

SKEER To move along quickly through narrow passage, touching boundaries at sides. (Wright)

SKILFER A fragment, splinter, little piece, became a term for dandruff; 1500s. (OED)

SKY-PARLOR A room at the top of a building, an attic, or a gallery on top level of a theater. (Davies)

SLOCKSTER A person who lured away another person's servants; 1684. (Mackay)

SLOPS Large trousers that supposedly were so overflowing with material that temporary seats were installed in the House of Commons during the reign of

Queen Elizabeth I to accommodate the wearers; 1500s–1600s. (Toone)

SLURG To be sleepy, lie around sluggishly; 1500s. (OED)

SLUT-GRATE The grating in the hearth through which ashes were emptied, leaving a small amount of cinders. (Wright)

SMERLES Ointment, from Old English *smyrels*; 1000–1340. (OED)

SMICK To kiss; a "Bagford Ballad" celebrated love by acknowledging, "You smack, you smick, you wash, you lick, you smirk, you swear, you grin"; 1570s–1600s (see introduction). (OED)

SMICKLY Fine, smart, from Danish *smykke* "to adorn," and Old English *smicer* "elegant." (Skeat)

SMOOR To smother. (Skeat)

SMOOTH-BOOTED Flattering, ingratiating so as to gain an advantage or a favor; 1500s–1700s (see introduction). (OED)

SNARP Keen, sharp; 1375. (OED)

SNIRP To pine, wither; also *snurpe*, as lamented in fourteenth-century poem "I snirp, I snobb, I sneip on snout" (see introduction). (Halliwell)

SNOOL To chide incessantly and destroy a person's spirit; to work so hard as to lose energy for living; also n. a pitiful person. (Mackay)

SNOOZLE To nestle, snuggle; also to settle in as do dogs. (Davies)

SNOUT-FAIR Fair-faced, handsome to point of becoming conceited, filled with self-importance; 1500s–1600s. (OED)

SOLIDUNGULOUS Whole-hoofed; complete. (McAdam)

SORN A corruption of *sojourn*, to sponge off, attach self to another to take advantage, eating and living from day to day in another person's home, unasked and unwelcome, stemming from long-standing practice of sheltering strangers seeking refuge from bands of armed men passing through the countryside and robbing people. (Mackay)

SOWL To pull by the ears. (McAdam)

SPISS Dense, thick; 1530–1800s. (OED)

SPOORN A phantom, a ghost; 1500s. (Halliwell)

STELLISCRIPT Writing in the stars, interpreted so as to predict fate; looking above one's head, one "read" from west to east to tell what good was yet to come, and from north to south to find out what evil to beware of; 1800s. (Davies)

STEWED PRUNES A term for brothel madams who kept these at their establishments as supposed preventives and cures for diseases contracted there, displaying the prunes on windowsills to indicate their places of business (see introduction). (Toone)

STIG To startle in alarm, from Old Norse *stygg-r* "shy, wary"; 1400s–1500s. (OED)

STILLICIDE The dripping of water, of particular importance in Scottish law regarding responsibility for dripping of rainwater from one house owner's eaves onto the land of another. (Shipley)

STILLWORTH Peaceful, perhaps related to *stalwart* from idea that a brave, valiant pose could lead to inner peace; 1275. (OED)

STOGGED Stuck, as in mud. (Davies)

STOO An exclamation meaning "Go! Go for it!" usually to urge hounds forward; 1600s. (OED)

STROAT To swell out, become puffed out, be filled full. (Skeat)

SUCKENY A smock, a coverup. (Shipley)

SUMMER-CASTLE A movable tower, elevated structure used often for protection during a siege; 1300s–1500s. (OED)

SUMMER'S BIRD A cuckold, an allusion to the migrating bird that appeared only during summer; 1500s–1600s. (OED)

SURPEACH An ornament of gold, silver, or jewels on a turban; 1700s–1800s. (OED)

SWEEK To swing; *sweek-bar* held pots and kettles in a fireplace; 1500s–1600s. (OED)

SWEVEN A dream, from Old English *swefn*. (Skeat)

SWINGLE To reel, become dizzy, giddy; 1000–1400. (OED)

CAISCH A phantom, a vision of a living person about to die or apparition of dead person come to life again; 1700s. (OED)

TALEVACE A large shield made of wood, from Old French *talevas*, itself an error in transposing two letters from Italian *tavolaccio* "a large table or wooden target," from Latin *tabula* "table"; 1400s. (OED)

TARTLE To hesitate, look at something dubiously as though not recognizing it. (Mackay)

TEALT Unsteady, shaky, also unreliable, as it applied to persons; 1000–1300s. (OED)

TEENFUL Troublesome, irritating, disturbing; 1000–1800s. (OED)

TENTIGINOUS Lascivious, inciting lust, from Latin *tentigo* "tenseness, lust"; 1600s–1700s. (OED)

THARM Intestines "twisted for several uses." (McAdam)

THEEK To cover a roof with straw thatch, to protect (a term still occasionally in use); 1300s on. (OED)

THODE A violent wind, a whirlwind; 700–1600s. (OED)

THRID To slide through a narrow passage. (McAdam)

THRUNCHED Very angry, displeased. (Mackay)

THUFTEN A maidservant, female slave; 1100–1200. (OED)

TIDDER To be prolific, produce many offspring; 1000–1250. (OED)

TIFLE To creep about, stir around; to create disorder by knocking something over. (Wright)

TIMWHISKY A tall, one-horse carriage for one or two people; also termed a *timmy-whisky*; 1700s–1800s. (OED)

TIRE-WOMAN A maker of women's headdresses, hats, caps, shortened from *attire*; 1600s. (Nares)

TOOTLE To try out notes under one's breath before going into full song. (Wright)

TOOZE To tease wool, drawing it out and plucking out imperfections, from Middle English *tosyn*; 1600s. (Skeat)

TUMBESTER A female tumbler or dancer; 1386–1400s. (OED)

TURKESS To alter something for the worse, to distort, twist; 1550–1600s. (OED)

TUTTING A tea-drinking get-together for women that, when opened to men, was followed by stronger drinks and wild behavior. (Halliwell)

TWATTER-LIGHT Twilight; 1600s. (OED)

TWISSLE The part of a tree trunk where branches separate; also one of a pair of apples or cherries attached to same stem. (Mackay)

𝒰NDER-BRIGHT The bright light that shines from behind clouds near the horizon. (Halliwell)

UNDERMEAL A light afternoon meal, from *undern* "time between noon and sunset." (McAdam)

UNPREGNANT Inept at business, unreceptive, unimaginative (see introduction). (Skeat)

UNPUCKER To smooth, relax. (Davies)

UNSNOD Rough, in disorder, not smooth to the touch. (Mackay)

URF A small, stunted, undersize child, later termed an *urchin*. (Mackay)

UTTER-WART A further, final warning. (Nares)

𝒱AFROUS Sly, cunning, crafty; 1500s–1700s. (OED)

VAMPERS Stockings or bottoms of socks attached to stockings, covering the foot more fully to keep feet and legs from getting wet. (Halliwell)

VATICIDE The murder of prophets or poets. (McAdam)

VEY To examine, inspect; 1512. (OED)

VIGIDITY Vegetation, fresh growth; 1628. (OED)

VOIDEE A fancy dish given to guests just before they left, consisting of wine with tidbits and spices; 1500s–1700s. (Shipley)

VOLO-NOLA Vacillating, wavering in making a decision, from Latin *volo* "I am willing" and *nolo* "I am unwilling"; 1600s. (OED)

VULT Countenance, facial expression, bearing, features of face; 1375–1600s. (OED)

𝒲ALKING-SUPPER A dinner in which the food selections were passed around the table for each person to carve or help himself to. (Halliwell)

WALMING Nausea, turning of the stomach; 1400s–1600s. (OED)

WAM A scar; 1000–1600s. (OED)

WANMOL Unable to use words effectively, not eloquent, unable to verbalize, from *moal* "speech." (OED)

WANWEIRD Ill fate, misfortune, from Old English *wyrd* "power to control events, destiny"; 1413–1800s. (OED)

WAPPER A lead ball attached to a strap used as a striking weapon; 1400s. (OED)

WATER-CASTER A person who inspected urine to diagnose disease; same as *piss-prophet*; 1600s–1800s. (OED)

WATER-GALL A dark rim around the eye after weeping; also a secondary, imperfectly formed rainbow indicating that more rain will follow, from Old English *gealew* "yellow." (Onions)

WATERGANG A trench for draining and channeling overflow of water; 1200s–1700s. (OED)

WAZE A cushion or bundle of straw placed at back of head. (Wright)

WEEZLE The windpipe, trachea; 1530–1770s. (OED)

WEMBLE To turn a cup upside down to signify having had enough tea. (Halliwell)

WHIFFLER An officer who preceded a procession, clearing the way and playing a wind instrument, from *whiffle* "to blow." (Toone)

WHITCH A hutch, chest, coffin, from Old English *hwicce* "an ark, coffer"; 1100–1600s. (OED)

WIDOW-BEWITCHED A woman separated from her husband. (Halliwell)

WIFTHING An affair outside of marriage, from Old English words for *wife* and *thing*; 1000–1200. (OED)

WINCHESTER GOOSE A sexually transmitted sore accompanied by swelling; term also for person thus afflicted and for a prostitute; in late sixteenth and seventeenth centuries, Bishop of Winchester had jurisdiction over public brothels near the Thames, where records show eighteen houses were in active use. (Shipley)

WITH A WET FINGER Easily, readily; Beaumont and Fletcher wrote that doing something *with a wet finger* was "as easy as turning pages in a book, rubbing out writing on a slate, or tracing a lady's name on a table with spilled wine"; 1600s–1700s. (Skeat)

WONDSOME Beset with difficulties, troublesome, difficult; 1400s. (OED)

WOOSE Marshy ground. (Davies)

WORBLE To wriggle, writhe; 1500s–1800s. (OED)

WORMSTALL An outdoor shelter for cattle to use in warm weather; 1600s–1700s. (OED)

WOWF Partially deranged. (Mackay)

WRAP-RASCAL A loose overcoat creating the impression of rakishness, also called a *hap-harlot*; 1700s–1800s. (OED)

WROX To begin to decay. (Mackay)

WURP A stone's throw; a glance of the eye; 1500–1600s. (OED)

*Y*ACK A blow to the head or ear. (Mackay)

YARNWINDLE A wooden device shaped like a cross for winding a skein of yarn into a ball, from Dutch *garenwinder*; 1300s–1800s. (OED)

YELLOW-BOY A gold coin, a guinea or sovereign; 1600s–1800s. (OED)

YELM A portion of straw that could be carried under one arm. (Mackay)

YERR To make a loud noise, yell, roar, cry out, howl; 1000–1450. (OED)

YOSKE To hiccup; 1400s–1500s. (Wright)

YOUNGHEDE A youth or youth in the abstract; 1200s–1300s. (OED)

YUX A hiccup. (McAdam)

*Z*OWERSWOPPED Ill-natured. (Wright)

· · · · · · · · · · · · ·

Davies, T. Lewis. *A Supplemental English Glossary.* London: George Bell and Sons, 1881.

Halliwell, James Orchard. *A Dictionary of Archaic and Provincial Words, Obsolete Phrases, Proverbs and Ancient Customs from the Fourteenth Century.* 2 vols. (first published 1847). London: Gibbings and Company, 1901; London: George Routledge and Sons, 1924 (7th ed.).

Mackay, Charles. *Lost Beauties of the English Language: An Appeal to Authors, Poets, Clergymen, and Public Speakers.* New York: Bouton, 1874.

McAdam, E. L., Jr., and Milne, George. *Johnson's Dictionary: A Modern Selection* (first published 1755). New York: Pantheon Books, 1963.

Murray, James A. H.; Bradley, Henry; Craigie, W. A.; and Onions, C. T. *The Oxford English Dictionary.* 12 vols. Oxford: Clarendon Press, 1933.

Nares, Robert. *A Glossary of Words, Phrases, Names, and Allusions in Works of English Authors, Particularly of Shakespeare and His Contemporaries.* London: George Routledge and Sons, 1905.

Onions, C. T. *The Oxford Universal English Dictionary.* 10 vols. New York: Oxford University Press—Doubleday Doran & Co., 1937.

Shipley, Joseph T. *Dictionary of Early English.* New York: Philosophical Library, 1955.

Skeat, Walter William. *A Glossary of Tudor and Stuart Words, Especially from the Dramatists.* Oxford: Clarendon Press, 1914.

Sperling, Susan Kelz. *Poplollies and Bellibones: A Celebration of Lost Words.* New York: Clarkson N. Potter, 1977.

———. *Tenderfeet and Ladyfingers: A Visceral Approach to Words and Their Origins.* New York: Viking Press, 1981.

Toone, William. *A Glossary and Etymological Dictionary of Obsolete and Uncommon Words.* London: William Pickering, 1832.

Wentworth, Harold. *American Dialect Dictionary.* New York: Thomas Y. Crowell Company, 1944.

Wright, Thomas. *Dictionary of Obsolete and Provincial English.* 2 vols. London: Henry G. Bohn, 1857.